INDIA UNDER NEHRU

INDIA UNDER NEHRU

S. JAGANNARAYANAN

MOTILAL BANARSIDASS
PUBLISHING HOUSE • DELHI
Email: naraina@mlbd.in • Website: www.mlbd.in
@mlbdofficial
+91 89 2999 9000

*2nd Reprint: Delhi, **2024***
First Edition: Delhi

ISBN: 978-93-5966-893-2 (Hardcover)
ISBN: 978-93-5966-097-4 (Paperback)

Printed & Published by
Rajendra P Jain *for*
Motilal Banarsidass Publishing House
A-44, Naraina Industrial Area, Phase I,
New Delhi–110 028 (INDIA)
Email: naraina@mlbd.in Website: www.mlbd.in
Tel.: (+91-11)4751 1592
Showroom:
4637/20, F-2, Hari Sadan, First Floor, Ansari Road, Daryaganj
Delhi–110 002 (Opp. Fire Station) ***Tel.***: (+91-11)4559 7999

Jawaharlal Nehru

DEDICATION

This book is dedicated to my Guru,
Shri T. T. Krishnamachari,
formerly Union Minister of Commerce and Industry,
Iron & Steel and Finance,
who nurtured me with affection and
who gave me the light of knowledge

and

to Shri Ranganathan, Padma Ranganathan and
Gayatri who treated me as a member of their family

and

to Shri T. S. Krishna, a symbol of
true friendship and affection,

and

to those Government servants –high and low,
working in the country and abroad,
who bore the brunt of toil with a cheerful heart
and to whom national pride and dedicated service
should be the living badge
in the manifold tasks awaiting them
in the Hundreds of Years to come.

T. T. Krishnamachari

INTRODUCTION

I have thought many times about the utility of adding one more book to the literature on Nehru. May be it is highly presumptuous on my part to attempt to write the guidelines of Mr. Nehru who had acted in a multi-sided way in the panorama of Indian history for the last 17 years. But I have my own reasons in defence of my decision to present this study before the public. The memory of Mr. Nehru and the impact of his work in various fields have impelled me to write what I feel about him not solely as a humble citizen and an ardent admirer, but also as a member of the Administration. In my view India was singularly blessed by the appearance of such a dynamic personality as Mr. Nehru and his continuing in office for a long period of 17 years after freedom. These were the years when one like me witnessed his performance inside and outside Government in the vast concourse of events both national and international. There have been many occasions for success, equally many occasions for regret, during the last 17 years. It could be argued that the decisions that were taken were not by one individual but they were collectively taken and the sole credit should, therefore, go to the group rather than to a single individual. These arguments have, no doubt, some validity but in the long perspective of things the major decisions that took place bore the impress of Mr. Nehru to a greater degree than any body else's. So, I soon found that my original attempt to trace only decisions solely belonging to Mr. Nehru proved sometimes a failure, but by and large, the impress of his personality was felt and traced on every occasion and on every national and international event.

A friend of mine asked me that in making an appraisal of the work done by Mr. Nehru a chapter should also be written about his omissions and mistakes. For instance, his decision to refer the Kashmir issue to the forum of the United Nations and our acceptance of plebiscite in Kashmir subject to certain conditions fulfilled by Pakistan and the subsequent refusal to hold the plebiscite for the solution of the Kashmir issue, as Pakistan had not fulfilled her obligations; and also the cession of territory which traditionally constituted as 'Tibet' to the Chinese, thereby annulling the old status of a buffer State which Tibet had enjoyed previously, had also been the subject-matter of severe criticism.

In some cases, the drawbacks arising from the present territorial formation of India based on linguism which has baffled solution of the national problem like food in the darkest times, such as we are having at present—a problem which requires India to be treated as one economic unit in spite of multi-State, zonal and territorial areas now constituting the frontiers of individual States—have served as a sharp reminder for reconsideration of the existing frontiers of the States. The same problem has also affected the mentality and core of the Services which have come to be talked of on linguistic lines instead of acquiring a national bias; and this is eating into the vitals of the Indian unity and the efficient performance of the administrative apparatus. In most of these cases it can be forcibly argued that Nehru being a towering personality could have avoided many such portents of evil. In the short distance of time and in the ever present contemporary nature of some of these problems we are apt to acquire a short term perspective instead of taking a long term view of things of some of these problems. Because they are essentially short term in implications, the remedies have also to be of a short term character and these problems, though they may appear to be very important and pressing in the immediate present, have been omitted from the survey of this book.

I have remained in Delhi in Central Service for the last 23 years and have had opportunities for closely watching the activities of the late Prime Minister, Pt. Jawaharlal Nehru with a keen interest and ardour. The memory of such a great person should be treasured by what I consider to be a feeble effort of a Government servant suffering from limitations of time and other equipment necessary to deal with such a big person and a big theme of the subject. If I have in any measure succeeded in bringing out the conflicts in his mind and the strains and stresses imposed in the climate in which he worked with singular zeal and with a number of institutions and personalities hovering around a single person as the 'Man of Decision', I feel I have done my work and have done a worthy job of it.

By way of acknowledgment I must express my deep gratitude to a number of persons whom I cannot individually mention, and their writings and also to the speeches and writings of Gandhiji, Jawaharlal Nehru, Rajen Babu, Dr. S. Radhakrishnan and a host of many other distinguished men of our contemporary times. I have also benefitted immensely from the writings and speeches of Shri T.T. Krishnamachari when he was a Central Minister and in some places I have even followed his concepts and language to give forceful expression and improve the form and content of this book, and also to the proceedings and debates of the Parliament and the Constituent Assembly of India and the publications of the Planning Commission.

I must also express my personal gratitude to Mr. Ghosh for helping me in the manuscript stage and to M/s. Sundarlal, Shantilal and Prakash, Proprietors of M/s. Motilal Banarsidass, Delhi-7, one of the foremost Oriental publishers and booksellers in the country, for assisting me in bringing out this book. The views expressed in this book are purely personal

New Delhi
17th November 1967. S. Jagannarayanan

CONTENTS

*

INDIA BETWEEN 1947 AND 1964
THE SEARCH FOR MR. NEHRU

Millions of words have been spoken and written of Mr. Nehru. He was the chosen man of Gandhi, and perhaps of God, to guide the destinies of India for a period of 17 years since India attained Independence. To the Indian and the foreigner, and to posterity, the role of Nehru in this momentous period of Indian history is something unique. In fact, after Gandhiji's death, in January, 1489, the governance of the country by Nehru came almost on the brink of a single man's rule and the world waited to see whether he would stick to the ideals which he had set before him and for which he had burnt himself in dedication before the attainment of freedom.

It is necessary to understand the historical perspective at the time of India's independence. Shattered by the World War II, the process of re-building and reconstruction of man, his heart and mind and his environment, was set in motion everywhere in the world. In Europe, the fabric of society had been crushed and the peace hungry peoples of Europe were groping in darkness to find out rays of amity and friendship between one nation and another. Massive economic aid was initiated by the benevolence of U.S.A. and the process of reconstruction was revived and accelerated. In the Far East and Africa the surge for freedom against colonial domination was rising and there were open protests against the White supremacy and against their discrimination on the basis of colour, creed and race. Alongside with the reconstruction of the environment began the process of rehabilitation of man as a human being. It was compassionately realised that man was born to live and let others live; and that the beast in him should be subordinated to the refined elements in him.

At this time of world history India got independence. It was on the 15th of August, 1947, that the three centuries of foreign domination of India came to an end. Yes, the foreign rule came to an end – with what great liabilities and arrears in human progress, mental, physical, economic and social backwardness. The partition of the country into Pakistan and India (Bharat) had left a deep car on the face of India with a crore of Indian population leaving Pakistan in the eastern and western borders in desolate hurry to safeguard their life and security. Internally, there was a breakdown of the law and order situation generated out of fear and distrust among the Muslim and non-Muslim sections of the society, and this situation was handled with firmness, thanks to the leadership of Mr. Nehru and Mr. Patel, Gandhi, C. R. and Maulana Azad and the efficiency of the Services.

The rehabilitation of the population was colossal in its dimensions requiring solution from an entirely humanistic angle. It involved the straining of resources, both men and material, to the utmost. A separate Ministry was created to look after the problems of the refugees and the properties left by them in Pakistan.

The leaders realised that no single step should be taken to loosen the bonds of the unity of India and the Governmental machinery. The setting up of the Constitution making body, which transformed itself into the normal legislature of the country at other times for enactment of statutes to carry on the day-to-day administration, was the next step towards directing the energies of the new India into the building task. The framers of the Constitution, especially the Drafting Committee and the members at large, had approached this problem with a singularly compassionate heart and improved on the situation by adopting various checks and balances found suitable to the *peculiar* political and social conditions in India.

The climate of harmony among the different sections of the population required the majority community to be generous and to some extent allow themselves to deny their rightful share in the privileges so that there might be a guarantee to the fear-ridden minorities for their safety and security and welfare and the dignity of their role in the body politic. A sense of confidence had to be created and the Christians, Muslims, Sikhs, Anglo-Indians and the diverse minorities and the faiths had to be persuaded to receive a fair deal in their aspirations. To the credit of the Sikhs and Christians, and due to the dexterity of the handling of the situation by the late Sardar Patel and Gandhiji, the minorities *themselves* came forward to drop their reservations and accept a fair chance at the hands of their brethren. This removal of distrust and promotion of understanding could not have taken place without the personal leadership of Gandhi, Nehru and Patel. The abolition of seperate electorates, the abolition of reservations for the minorities in the Constitution, a willingness to take a chance in the political and economic ordeals of the life in the country, was the first surest step towards preserving the communal harmony in the country. If this had not been done, today we could not have seen Zakir Hussain, Dr. Cherian, Jag Jiwan Ram, Kakkan, Sanjeevaya and others occupying high positions in the State to which they have risen on their own. All this was possible because people had great confidence in the policy and leadership of Mr. Nehru.

The framers of the Constitution not only embodied provisions of the Fundamental Rights and the Directive Principles in the Constitution, but also displayed a keen sense of far-sightedness in the future administration of these provisions which they regarded as the sheet-anchor of the safety and security of the minorities. For instance, the nomination principle introduced in the Constitution and the absence of discretion to the President for appointment of Governors of the States instead of on an election basis enshrined a noble principle that the problem of the minorities should be dealt with by a combination of mind and heart, by the right choice of a person in whom the minorities can have confidence. Again, the setting up of the office of the Election Commissioner as an independent organ and defining its role in the Constitution free from executive control was another step taken towards promotion of communal harmony. It should be remembered that to this body has been transferred the functions of superintending, directing and controlling the preparation of the electoral rolls and the conduct of all elections to the Parliamentand the State Legislatures. This body has been, therefore, the fountain base of the Indian democracy. Its conduct and performance should be above board.

The Services are compared to the artery system

of modern Government. Without an efficient Service apparatus, the writ of the Government cannot run in the remote corners of the country. In the British days the Services acquired a great reputation for loyalty, efficiency and objectivity. There was also the implicit obedience arising out of strict discipline born of suspicion by the foreign Government itself. The main function of the British rule for the last three centuries had been to maintain law and order. In this climate, the Services were fostered with the greater emphasis on maintenance of law and order than on other functions like developmental functions, etc. of the State.

As soon as the country attained Independence, a great strain was imposed on the Services because of the immediate and pressing need to maintain the balance between law and order on the one hand and the developmental functions on the other. The Indian Civil Service which constituted the core of the Civil Services has often been compared in the to an 'iron bowl' supplied to the Indian leaders prison. Just as the 'bowl' was used for various purposes by the leaders in the prison, so also the Indian Civil Service officers were used for a variety of services. Mahatma Gandhi and other leaders redefined the role of the Services as servants of the people as against their previous role as custodians of the law and order situation. The officers also accepted the changed character of their functions and proved in no way inferior to the other sections of the community in respect of patriotism and service to the country during a critical period following 1947 and afterwards.

The Services were fortified in their role to play a useful part in the country's development because of the assurance given to them initially by the leaders and later embodied in the Constitution. The creation of the independent and impartial organisation like the Union Public Service Commission safeguarded the interests of the Services and relieved them of their just fear in respect of recruitment, promotion and disciplinary code of behaviour. In a democratic country like India where the leaders are liable to be changed by a system of the five year period of elections, the frequent changes in the Ministerial personnel or their portfolios imposed a serious challenge on the utility of the Services to the country. The Ministers chosen from the public are not generally accustomed to an expert knowledge of methods of Government in matters of high finance and industry which in modern days have become a specialised subject due to fast-moving economic forces in the country and abroad; and they needed the guidance of expert administrators in matters of policy formation and detailed working. In this way the Services provided an element of stability to the economic governance of the country. In a democratic federal set-up of a country like India, the 'planning' functions also gave then a new scope for the outlet of their energies and many world organisations like the United Nations, the World Bank, have commended very highly about the quality and integrity of the Indian Civil Service officers.

The Indian Foreign Service, mostly recruited from the then existing Indian Civil Service Officers, was also started from scratch. It is now a fullgrown adult and is able to grow and make its impact in the fields of international diplomacy and international trade.

With the intensification of the Plan schemes, there has been a growing need for intensifying the expert knowledge of 'economic administrators'. The problems of trade, high finance and credit control and the fostering of industrial growth and management of public sector undertakings, require not only the expert knowledge but also a continuity in tradition and outlook. The Services have to preserve an all-India character and impart an element of stability in the administrative cohesiveness of the country and in the enforcement of its writ from time to time. The Indian Civil Service officers belonged to a compact group of administrators, keen and efficient, and were capable of performing as many duties as possible. They rose to the needs of the occasion and there was a complete transformation of their mental attitude and they placed the service motive before themselves in the administration of the country. In fact, without the help of these officers the administration of this vast country in the changed circumstances would have been very difficult. The assurance to the Services that their rights and privileges would be preserved and later this assurance finding a place in the written Constitution of India, was also due to the personal leadership of Mr. Nehru and Patel.

The principle of one adult, one vote was also adopted as the basis of electoral qualification. This principle of adult franchise has released the plentitude of opportunity for every Indian to whatever sect, creed or religion he may belong, to attain his rightful role in the body politic. To a large extent, it has shattered the chances of the privileged classes *to continue* to govern the weaker elements of the society. To this extent it has strengthened the hopes and faith which the minorities and the common people had in Mr. Nehru. The rise of Shri Kamaraj and Shri Lal Bahadur Shastri from humble beginnings are illustrations of the working of democracy in India.

The adoption of the National Emblem, National Flag, the National Anthem, the National Song, the National Calender and the National Dress has quickened the process of emotional integration of India. The centrifugal forces were to some extent re-asserting after the States' reorganisation on the basis of linguistic principle, but soon it was realised that the common language in the shape of Hindi was to bind the links together, and towards this end, efforts are being continued.

The planning technique introduced by Mr. Nehru for ameliorating the economic and social backwardness of the people has helped to complete the process of unification of India into a single fabric. In fact, the setting up of the Planning Commission as an instrument of unifying agency came towards the end of February, 1950, that is, a month after the promulgation of the Indian Constitution. But during the intervening period, from 1947 to 1950, and again for the first few years after the Republican Constitution came into force, the work of centralisation had to be brought into being and initially the States were asked to accept the laws passed by the Centre in respect of powers to deal with production, supply and distribution etc. of essential commodities. In a country like India where the size and the number of the population are considerable, and where sufficient production has not been established in food and essential goods, the trend towards the Centre attracting greater powers from the States in the process of integration was not avoidable. In the modern India where planning will have to be resorted to for the mobilisation of resources and effective distribution of the produced goods to all levels of population and the remote corners such economic intervention by the Centre will have to be a necessary concomitant with a view to achieve the economic objectives of the Indian Constitution which have been embodied in the Directive Principles. If the residuary powers, vested with the Centre by the Constitution, had been solely relied upon for such intervention it would be necessary to justify every time for Governmental action and public interest would not be served at all times and on every occasion, and many practical difficulties would arise; even the period of intervention might be in jeopardy. For instance, in respect of schemes like the DVC, the Drugs Regulation and many such schemes, requiring uniformity of action and affecting the interests of more than one State, the Articles 249-253 of the Constitution would have to be invoked and every time some *co-ordination* of action in such matters which requires enabling provisions for the Centre to interfere in avowedly State Subjects—not to speak of the Concurrent Subjects—was considered necessary. Obviously, later, to obviate these difficulties, the Planning Commission was set up in 1950 as an independent body and the link between the Centre and the States was forged through the National Development Council at which the Chief Ministers of all the States were present.

A large measure of success attended on Mr. Nehru's efforts of unification of the country as he was virtually the head of the Congress Party which controlled ministries in almost all the States for a long period. It was thus possible for him, and through him for the Ruling Party, to give a new turn and accelerate the goal of attainment in the economic growth of the country. The discussions in the open Party meetings helped Mr. Nehru to get the approval of the people for Governmental policies which also involved changes in the methods of working of the Governmental machinery and re-defining the objectives of the economic policy of the Government. In fact, it was in January 1950, at a meeting of the Congress Working Party Committee, that the decision was taken to constitute the Planning Commission. The same Congress Party widened the scope of the planning to cover the goal of the attainment of the socialistic pattern of society as a result of the discussions of the Avadi Congress in 1956. Thus, Nehru jockeyed on the twin house of Governmental machinery and the Party and drew the support of the one to fashion the policies of the other. For instance, when the planning problems arose he used the forum of the National Development Council at which the Chief Ministers were present. The influence which the National Development Council, the Planning body and the Party acquired over 17 years was in a large measure due to Nehru's *personal* leadership. In fact, at one of the first meetings of the National Development Council in 1952 he stressed that all the Chief Ministers bore intimate responsibility for the Plan in all its phases. Thus, he exhorted them to look upon every question from a national point of view and at every stage he worked for the *national consensus* and he exhorted the States to work under the shadow of that consensus.

Later, in 1956 and 1962 and 1965, when India was subject to external aggression from China and Pakistan, the policy of national unity was put to a heavy strain. But the country and the people bore the new responsibility with redoubled vigour and for the success of meeting these challenges credit must be given to the foreign and defence policies pursued by Mr. Nehru. Today, the conception of nationalism has become so much sophisticated that Indians in foreign countries inevitably form a national group and hang together for various purposes inspite of their internal differences. For instance, the Indians in a foreign land would be termed as Indians to whatever State in India they might belong to. A status has thus been created for the Indians abroad during the regime of Mr. Nehru. In all these acts one cannot fail to notice the trend towards national unity the seeds of which had been sown in Mr. Nehru's time.

With the help of the Planning technique Nehru wanted to introduce changes in the individual and technological structure of the society by emphasising the role of science and the scientific method on a larger scale and by promising a self-reliant economy which within itself would possess the means of achieving rapid economic growth and solve urgent social problems. Technology in India required to be oriented with reference to the needs of the situation. The enormous scientific and technological developments that had taken place in the West, especially the U.S.A., the U.S.S.R., West Germany and Japan, had induced India to invite and attract the flow of scientific thought from all countries without any distinction. At the same time, the absorption capacity of India had to be enlarged so that the resources could be tapped to the extent necessary to keep pace with the inflow of technical knowledge and foreign capital. Simulataneous with the appointment of the Planning Commission in 1950 was also the constitution of the Scientific Manpower Committee. This laid the basis for the remarkable advance of scientific and technical education in the later years to come. The immediate results were the setting up of a chain of laboratories on a national scale, the setting up of the Department of Atomic Energy over which Nehru himself presided and the opening of a number of technical institutes in collaboration with the foreign countries at various places in India. As a result of these steps, the training of Indians in new fields in India and abroad was given a momentum. These efforts of India were helped by the offers of economic and technological aid from the various countries as a result of friendly attitude towards all the nations.

These 17 years were also an intense period of building friendly ties with foreign countries for which sole credit should be given to Mr. Nehru. The period of isolation and subjugation to which India had been condemned for several *centuries* had crippled India's spiiitual potentialities and economic prosperity. The task of rebuilding the nation based on the fund of goodwill and understanding and friendly relationship of foreign countries was by no means an easy task. It required the strengthening of the Ambassadorial ties and the setting up of the Embassies and Missions in outside countries. A number of men of culture had to be sent abroad to interpret India's needs on the one hand and the policy of her friendship with all on the other. The foreign policy of India was also shaped to suit the ideals of peace at home and abroad, and international amity. It was laid on the sure foundations of disarmament, strengthening of the United Nations as a forum for resolving the differences among the nations, and nuclear ban. The slowly diminishing tension and the fading out of the clouds of cold war weakened the basis of military blocks and the emergence of a third 'neutral force' consisting of non-aligned nations, due to the indefatigable efforts of Mr. Nehru, was a decisive factor for the survival of mankind. As Russell had said, "Had India foregone the non-alignment it is seriously doubtful that other nations could have maintained it and the area of conflict would be more." "Peace and freedom are indivisible. The world cannot be partly free and partly subject. So also prosperity. There are always new ways and new ideas with which we can change our horizons; we shall see the old; this is our heritage. But we shall also see the new; this is our future. (Nehru—Discovery of India). With this breath of warmth and friendship, the infant independent India received goodwill visits from all the Heads of Governments to India. Thus, the neutral policy has resulted in the enormous potentialities of trade with all the countries, particularly the U.S.S.R. and the East European countries. To some extent, our neutralism tempered with an attitude to judge all international issues with *objectivity* annoyed the U.S.A. and the U.K. many times; and at the time of the Suez Canal crisis, our pro-Egypt attitude incurred the wrath of the U.K. and even led to the resignation of Mr. Eden as the Prime Minister of England. Apart from these strange incidents, we benefitted by and large, from this mental approach which strengthened the moral foundations of our external policy.

India's decision to stay within the Commonwealth represented India's desire to continue the friendly ties between the U.K. and India. This was a history-jolting decision for India. The whole world was gazing at India what she would do after she attained independence. Consistent with India's Republican status, Mr. Nehru made Parliament agree to a status which would make India a Republic and at the same time completely independent and sovereign, owing no allegiance to the King as the other Commonwealth countries did owe. India would however agree to Commonwealth membership as a symbol of free partnership or association with the King (not the crown) ;and in this relationship the King has no functions. This is a novel idea. something like creating a new status between completetly being foreign and being of one nationality. As Mr. Nehru stated, while moving the resolution in Parliament on 10th May, 1949, the objective has been to reach the highest measure of understanding, not the lowest measure of agreement. India desired to maintain all links with other countries as did not come in the way of her freedom of action and independence. It was a novel type of association with a healing touch, forgetting the bitter past. As Nehru said, "I think it is not a safe thing to encourage to break up any association that anyone has in this world of disruptive forces."

The underlying motive was to maintain links with the other countries without inhibiting our freedom. Through the window of Commonwealth membership India peeped outside; and worked for the welfare and free association of the individual ations and the promotion of world peace.

This spirit of understanding was in a measure derived from Gandhiji's tutorship. Gandhiji stated : "While I hold the British rule to be a curse, I do not intend harm to a single Englishman or to any legitimate interest that he may have in India." This novel theory of association or partnership assuaged the misgivings about India's sudden change of administration. It also protected the British commercial and industrial interests in the country and this attitude formed the basis of the Industrial Policy in 1948, 1949, and again in 1956 which gave guarantee to the foreign interests at the time of a cry of nationalisation.

India had gained immensely from British rule. It inherited a closely-knit British Indian territory served by a very efficient administrative apparatus. The Parliamentary system of Government was based on the English principle of equality before law and jurisprudence.

Mr. Nehru preached for the elevation of the conscience of world humanity and common brotherhood. As he has once said, "After all, in the dealings with the nations, it is ultimately the mind and the heart that matters and if the mind narrows down, the heart becomes full of bitterness and freedom becomes blurred and absurd, justice threatened and there is chaos in the world. Therefore, freedom and peace are indivisible. It involves not only the claim of the individual to grow but also of a nation to make the best use of the capacity of its people in the international sphere." In this way the importance of emancipation of Asian and African countries was initiated and a policy of co-existence and tolerance among the peoples of the world was proclaimed as the best formulation for world peace and progress. This approach reflected a democratic ideal and translated in the sphere of mind tolerance not only for those who agreed with us but also for those who would not agree with us. It also projected the concept of a higher democracy based on a national franchise in the international sphere. Democracy is not only political, not only economic but also something of the mind. It involves not only equality of opportunity in the political and economic domains but also a certain amount of tolerance for the less progressive nations of the world. In our dealings we are apt to forget human values and human standards. Life is a big and multi-faced affair. Ultimately, man is a human animal and if human values go, the graciousness of life also departs. Then it does not make much difference as to what happens to life afterwards. (Nehru—San Francisco, 1949).

Thus, the foreign and defence policies pursued by the Indian Government under Nehru presented a concept of national unity to the world abroad. The programme of the Indian National Government in its external relationship was fortified by Gandhian traditions of amity and friendship and non-violence, and our angular approach in the context of our internal and external affairs was on many occasions corrected and a sense of "national outlook" was developed on many issues. At present there is no likelihood of giving up this process and all this has happened because of Mr. Nehru's stewardship of the Foreign Affairs Ministry in addition to his being the Prime Minister of the country and the Head of the Party. He has worked hard on the thin threads of the divisive forces and evolved out of them a background of unity and nationalism rooted in the past and at the same time the eyes turning towards the future. He built a new fabric of India with a multi-sided institutional support and committed the Indians to an orderly form of Government with a deep agricultural background which had in the pre-Independence days knit the people together in a very loose way. This background was a mixture of philosophy, tradition, history, myth and legend and was woven into the future with a hope and faith for social and economic amelioration. In this background he toiled also very hard to give a new status to the Indian women. The Special Marriage Act, 1954, could be described as a uniform civil code of marriage and a step towards a uniform civil code for all citizens contemplated by the Constitution. Those coming under its provisions will be Indians governed by a uniform law of marriage though belonging to different religions. A Hindu or a Muslim marrying under it, for he ceases to be governed by his personal law in important matters, will now cease to be a Hindu or a Muslim. There was no doubt much opposition to this kind of communal legislation by a secular State which tried to avoid steps to reform Muslim Law. The real answer for this kind of objection was that India had a multitude of conflicting laws based partly on Hindu law and partly on Muslim law.

The British tried to introduce uniform and equal laws applicable to all citizens. Secularism and equality were introduced in the laws codified or otherwise administered by the British rulers. At any rate, a beginning had been made for liberalising reforms in the field of marriage and divorce. The widow of the Hindu was not only made a co-sharer in the property of her husband along with her sons but also the daughter in a family was elevated to the statusrof a son, in the share of her father's properties. The right of divorce was upheld as much as the right of women for equal wages for equal work along with men was affirmed in the Constitution. All these social reforms led to the awakening of the down-trodden sections of the Indian community; and the planners gave support to these sections by welfare schemes in the plans. The women of India occupy high positions (Governor, Prime Minister, Chief Minister, administrator) in the body politic. They have been enabled to share with men in every way the privileges of citizenship. Judged by the progress of women, as Mr. Nehru remarked while agreeing with a French writer on the discussion of Hindu Succession Bill in 1956, the hall-mark of a civilized society is the opportunity given for women. The new India witnessed a silent and sturdy growth of the nationalism rooted in the past.

The programme of the Indian National Government included the priority of other social reforms. As an instance in point towards equality we have to cite the Fundamental Rights in the Constitution in favour of secularism. Many of us would unhesitatingly answer that the provision which abolishes untouchability and forbids its practice gives powerful support to the secular attitude as it helps to rid the country of a social evil which has sprung out of certain religious practices. No doubt, the loyalties of caste and community had been ingrained for centuries in the minds of the mass of the community and on this account the efforts made by the State for preserving secular attitude in the minds of the population were laudable. Only a sustained and effective cooperation between the State and the citizens with a clear bias towards secularism can wear off these narrow sectional loyalties.

At present, all citizens, male or female, high-born or low-born, have been enabled to participate in every way in the privileges of citizenship and the governance of the country. The fruits of the partition had been reaped;the doubts of Indian nationality have been set at rest. A status for Indian citizenship has been created in the country and abroad. The new nationality that has come as a result of these changes is not based on religion or on communal considerations. The word "Indian" represents today that synthesis of citizenship derived essentially from the Indian philosophic outlook with the urge for development on the social, economic, political and cultural planes. It was a challenge to our historical culture, but the challenge was met successfully by a new synthesis and a process of absorption. This process has within it a peculiar genius, the seeds of rejuvenation and will soon sprout forth new blossoms of culture, the background and the essential moorings of the past remaining the same.

What is the dimension of opportnnity for the new Indian citizen released by the forces of the integration for which Mr. Nehru has set the pace? Today, a Punjabi or a Sikh can settle in Madras for livelihood in the same way that a Southerner can come to Delhi and work under the vaults of the Secretariat. The Muslim of Bengal or U. P. can move without fear to Bombay and follow his occupation without any restriction. The Assamese can have the services of the residents of other provinces without any fear of parochialism. As time goes on this kind of national outlook and cultural homogeneity may deepen and the ideals of unity will receive a further impetus.

The new synthesis which we witness in the youth of India is perhaps the greater contribution of Nehru. The youth of today are inspired by the tremendous work he has done and the vast gap of his residual work which is beckoning them. The new spirit of freedom and creative energy is abroad. This new spirit and creative energy requires to be harnessed in desired fields of national integration and advancement. He once said of himself: "There is the ambition left in me and it is this that in the years to come and in the few years left to me, I should throw myself with all the strength and energy left in me into the work of building up India. I want to do it to the uttermost, till I have exhausted my energies and strength in India's task. I do not care what happens to my reputation after I am gone. But if any people chose to think of me, then I should like them to say, 'this was a man who with all his mind and heart loved India and the Indian people, and they in truth were indulgent to him and gave him their love most abundantly and extravagantly." (Kalyani Session of the Congress). Looking at India in the Historical Perspective, he stated, "What is my inheritance?.........To all that humanity has achieved during tens of thousands of years, to all that it has thought and felt and suffered and taken pleasures in, to the cries of triumph and its bitter agony of defeat, to that astonishing adventure of man which began so long ago and yet continues and beckons to us. To all this and more, in common with all men. But there is a special heritage for those of us in India not exclusively to me, for none is exclusive and all are common to the race of man, the more especially applicable to us, something that is the flesh and blood and bones that has gone to make us what we are and what we are likely to be."

This new synthesis of India has a rational appeal as opposed to the old theory of destiny and resignation to fate. He, the modern Indian, has also the virtues of tolerance, tolerance not only of those who agree with him but also of those who do not agree with him. He is not forgetful of human values and human standards. He enjoys the freedom of speech, association and expression. He respects the rule of law. He is willing to learn the finer and deeper sides of human life in the world and might be said to represent the conscience of the world community. By the institution of adult franchise, Nehru has made every Indian to articulate politically on all issues concerning India and the wo ld. Thus, the umbrella of his regime gave protection for the individual freedom to grow and made the best use of his abilities. The rule of law signifies an institution, not a slogan. Courts are independent. He is willing to pay taxes and pay penalties for default. He is prepared to behave as a decent law-abiding citizen.

II

THE INDIAN REPUBLIC

January 26, 1950—a day of momentous significance for India and the Indian people. They were fortunate to witness the emergence of a new star of the Republic of India and their successors may envy this day. The star of a free India beckoned us forward with a mighty man of destiny at the helm of affairs, namely, Pandit Jawaharlal Nehru. When he resumed office as the Prime Minister in the Republican Constitution, the country was burdened with a heavy carry-over of problems unheard of in the history of several countries. Never before in the distant past of Indian history had such a vast expanse of Indian territory come under one single authority. We had heard of spiritual leaders like the Buddha, Sankara and Rāmānuja, who dominated the minds of the inhabitants of the Indan sub-continent in the distant past in the spiritual sphere, but never in the Regal history including the period of Ashoka, such a single individual had wielded so much love and authority as Pt. Jawaharlal Nehru over such a vast area. How was this battle won ? This was fought and won without *arms*, and without much waste of resources. Nehru had a great leader in Gandhi who inspired the masses and the intellegentsia. We had other leaders too, but it was the mass of the country who bore the brunt of the struggle and they had supreme faith in Pt. Jawaharlal Nehru.

The country at that time was disfigured by communal tensions and ugly incidents leading to a large exodus of Hindus from Pakistan and our resources and administrative energies were bent on rehabilitating those unfortunate victims into suitable occupations. Side by side with the need for arriving at a satisfactory communal pact with Pakistan we had also the problem to reach an agreement with them for restoring normal trade channels and evolving a satisfactory solution forthe problem of evacuee properties.

On the political side the work of re-constructing India into a single political entity was initiated and completed by the indefatigable energies of Sardar Patel. The integration of the Indian States was completed and in India's history over a period of thousand years we had a giant territory extending from Kashmir to Cape Comorin and from Gujarat to Kamrup, brought under one system. For such a mighty work there were many difficulties like the intransigence of some rulers, the parochial attitude displayed by other ruling princes and the absence of a well-knit political organisation in some Indian States. But all these problems were evercome and the political transformation of India into one unit was accomplished with the helpful attitude and co-operation by some of the ruling princes of the big States. What could have been the reason for such a new process ? The underlying current of affinity which bound the Indian rulers and the Indian masses and the political leaders to come to a sense of mental tolerance had created a feeling of oneness—a feeling that they belonged to a rich heritage and that they have been chosen by God to fulfill the noble purpose in life in the years to come. This discovery of oneness gave a new turn and a new direction in the purpose of Indian life. The political leaders were no longer anarchists defying the old British laws and courting imprisonment. Their usefulness to the society in the new set of circumstances, their responsibility as rulers after the independence came to be judged by the kind of political and economic conscience that prevailed in the political situation of the country and the manner in which that situation educated its men and institutions. For the first time in their life, the 'Congress rebels" found themselves as rulers and they had a moral responsibility for the efficient governance of their country. They realised that they had to bequeath to the posterity an India where an unlimited toil passing from one generation to another for completing the nation's work was awaiting. The political leaders also realised that vital energy was visible everywhere, even in the remote villages of the country, from the highest to the lowest quarters of Governmental activity; and this vital energy mnst be tapped to create new fields of activity and open new avenues for their genius. The governance of a multi-lingual and a multi-regional country required the widest measure of tolerance and evolution of a democratic policy to suit not only the political and economic needs of the country but also strengthen the defence and foreign relationship with countries abroad in the years to come.

Gandhiji laid stress on the purity of methods while Nehru worked out for the loftiness of the nation's policy. The zeal with which Nehru worked on the legacy of Gandhi during the period of transition of India from foreign domination and later during the period of consolidation and reform must surely be attributed to the personal leadership of Mr. Nehru and his discipleship with Gandhiji. The path of progress of a country lay not merely in exploiting and overcoming the deficiencies of thepeople's characteristics but also willfully and conscientiously working hard and making a path inspite of various difficulties towards common objectives based on a moral and friendly spirit. During his wanderings in the country in the early part of his career Nehru had seen the anguished peasant's face in India. The peasants looked on him with loving and hopeful eyes as though he would be the bearer of good advice and a messanger of hope and relief. The new picture of India Nehru visualised before him was not the picture of a mere starving and miserable peasant, that casual visitor from distant city, who embarassed him but a *hopeful* citizen that filled Mr. Nehru with new responsibilities, that sometimes frightened him. After Gandhiji had led the revolution of Indian independence to success by peaceful methods, Nehru built that edifice upon the sure foundations of devotion to social and economic progress, reforms of social rights etc. An intellectual product of the Western civilisation, he tried to impart a new outlook of science and technological progress to the urges of the spirit and the mind of the people.

How did he start about the work of re-constructing the way of Indian living ? The path of peace which had been shown by Gandhiji, Nehru strictly adhered to. He tried to evolve a policy of peace and friendship—peace not only inside the country but peace with all the neighbours and the sister countries of the world.

The first phase of integration and consolidation

was over and the country was on the onward march towards the re-building task. For such a mighty work there were many handicaps. The population was growing at the rate of five percent per year. The country was studded with innumerable small units of manufacture engaged in a variety of consumer goods with inefficient standards of technology. These small units were unable to grow because there were no fixed markets for them and they were actually deteriorating because the large-scale industries were their chief competitors. The war of 1939 had witnessed the growth of steel and textiles, but barring these industries, industrial structure could by no means be regarded as a well-developed one. There was no industrial policy as such for the growth and dispersal of industries over the regions of India. The Government had a scheme of discriminating protection, mostly one-sided, to help the foreign imports raher than the indigenous industrial growth. Foreign capital still counted for majority of ownership and management, and more than 30 per cent of the paid-up capital of all joint stock owners was under foreign control. The important tertiary industries like banking, insurance, shipping, transport. and railways, were in the hands of the foreigners The major export industries like the plantations were also owned by foreigners. Indians were not given an effective role in the management of foreign-owned companies and the employment of Indians in the equivalent of managerial and technical executive posts was very meagre. After Independence, the fear of nationalisation of foreign ownership was common to both the foreign capitalists and to the shy Indian entrepreneurs. There was no public or private sector industries. The employment potentialities and the opportunities were at the lowest ebb. There was no scientific dispersal of industries. The major industries like textiles, had been mostly concentrated in four towns, namely, Bombay, Kanpur, Calcutta and Madras. There was no scientific survey made by Government or by any private organisation of the available resources for any kind of planning in India. Indian labour was teeming in millions mostly unskilled and with a lower productivity.

In this climate our objectives had to be clearly defined. While moving the Objectives Resolution in the Constituent Assembly on December, 13, 1946, Mr. Nehru stated, "Although in this Resolution we have not used the word 'democratic' because we thought it obvious that the word 'Republic contains the meaning of the word...we have given the content of democracy not only the content of political democracy, but also the content of economic democracy." The appointment of the Planning Comission in 1950, one month after the promulgation of the Republican Constitution was a positive policy to develop in the right direction. The State governments were regarded as the agency for the implementation of the plan in regard to agriculture, power and road schemes. The Central Government formulated draft plans which were placed before the National Development Council and the Parliament for approval. They also took upon themselves certain tasks like the opening and enlargement of the Public Sector and some multi-purpose projects, the administration of which required theco-operation of more than one State. These plans were mostly based on either resources available or facilitiesalready developed at that period of time in various locations. As a matter of fact, no survey of resources had been made for any kind of scientific planning nor the facilities developed in advance with a view to make any scheme of the Centre or the State a succussful venture. The choice of sites was the subject of several considerations sometimes uneconomic, sometimes political. With such a background of development of non-resources and non-facilities based schemes, the economic and social over-heads were bound to be excessive and an appraisal on a profit or loss basis for some of these projects was untenable purely on cost considerations or on economic factors.

In the initial years of Republican democracy, Nehru contributed to its successful working to a great measure. Internally, he organised three elections based on adult franchise with all the ideals of democratic principles through opposition parties also operating. The elections were carried on to the remotest corners of the village in this vast area of land and covered 170 million voters and more than 3,500 seats to be filled in the Central and State Legislatures. The contesting parties were given freedom to canvass their own candidates and the freedom of press was by and large upheld. The emergence of opposition parties which would have as their fundamental aim the fighting of elections was no doubt a sufficient incidental guarantee against the possibility of lust for power by the ruling party. Even the communists were allowed to function within the framework of the Constitution and the concept of "loyal opposition" was what the Indian situation required at that moment. The political arena required an in-built set-up in which the Indian political parties would act within the broad framework of the Constitutional democracy while questioning the methods of the ruling Government. In the last analysis, the ultimate claim of a democratic authority is that it permits dissent and survives it.

The institution of adult franchise, the vast area and the numbers that inhabit the territory of India and the graded inequalities in the social and economic spheres inherited by the Republic of India from distant past and the presence of different ideologies of peoples in the comity of international sphere were likely to mislead the energies of the infant India into wrong channels. So long as Nehru was alive it was possible for him to lead the Government and also simultaneously head the Party which formed the Government in the Centre as well as in the States. After his death this kind of dual control both of the Party and the Governments at the Centre and the States would possibly become weak and the pair of arms, namely, the Party and the Government would require the supplementary efforts of one or the other for their strength. In a Parliamentary democracy the weakness of the one may weaken the other. Perhaps to avoid this kind of weakening influences setting in, Nehru has sought to evolve a system of checks and balances and plan for the constitutional growth of this country.

For instance, the application of detention rules without trial of some anti-national and anti-social elements that India witnessed during certain emergency periods and during the breakdown of law and order situation and the consequent promulgation of Governor's rule, must be construed in the context as cautious steps of the Central Government to forge the ideas of unity and adherence to the principles of Indian Constitution based on Indian nationalism. Similarly, the incarceration of some of the anti-national leaders and the suppression of the activities of those parties which base their faith on communal principles must also be viewed negatively as the Centre's punitive measures to curb excessive anti-nationalism and anti-secularism, and positively build up in the country elements in the Opposition parties of loyalty to the basic principles of the Indian Constitution. The periodical approval and sanction of the Indian Parliament for the administration of the Preventive Detention Act showed Nehru's continued faith in democratic principles of governing the country. The country was, no doubt, undergoing new experiences in the "emergence" of Opposition parties rooted in the fundamental principles governing the party system. While the future is unpredictable, the process of alignment of parties rooted on certain basic principles is going on until such time the "loyal" opposition ideal is fostered. The ruling Government, to whatever party they may belong would have to act with firmess in putting down anti-national and anti-secular and anti-social activities.

What is the future of Indian Democracy ? The democratic political method has successfully operated over a period of years and must be presumed to change the character of the conflict that can take place within the society. On this basis, the future of Indian democracy depends upon whether the democratic political method borrowed from the West and transplanted on the Indian soil with adult franchise as the basis of election and the opposition parties still in the mould of formation, can change the character of the conflict that is taking place slowly and imperceptibly in the Indianbody politic during the last 17 years under Nehru's stewardship. Hitherto the scope of conflict was restricted to regional differences, communal differences, unequal partnership in economic prosperity and graded social inequalities resulting in the denial of freedom and economic opportunity to the weaker sections of the Indian body politic, especially in the context of the colossal arrears of human progress in the fields of literacy, health and social outlook. These differences were also intensified on account of language differences and social inertia and immobility and lack of communication and modern methods of travel. Now, when the planning process which Nehru has initiated is intensified, some of these communal differences are bound to disappear while certain new problems like regional differences based on material inequality are bound to crop up in the years to come. In other words, there will be imperceptibly a shift in the character of political conflict from communal differences to new alignments based on economic factors such as inequalities in material prosperity of certain States and regions. So long as it is possible to bring unity within the parties, one primary aim of democratic socialism will have been fulfilled. Only through the institution of the parties, it is possible to achieve balanced growth of the federal structure without upsetting the climate for national unity which has been created in the last seventeen years Shri Rajagopalachari's efforts in the role of a dissenter are praiseworthy in this context.

It should be borne in mind that the intensification of the Plan process weakens the federal structure as the powers of the Central Government are becoming vast. But it would be in this process that the destructive divisive forces in the country may get dwindled and disappear in the course of years. At the same time, the role of the States in the changed atmosphere will also undergo a radical change. In a federal structure like India, the States have a vital part to play. They should not be allowed to lose their individuality and dignity and genius. On the other hand, strong leadership in the State may upset this kind of balance and the centrifugal tendencies may assert. Here lies the strength of the party. Democratic leaders of the party can hold powers at the Centre so long as the party is able to maintain power both at the Centre and the States.

A strong party can build up political systems both in the Centre and the States. The Governments do not produce science, philosophy, music and literature. These important human excellences are achieved elsewhere and it is from this point of view that the merit of democracy should in the end be considered. The vitality of the people is created out of human excellences; and these qualities are self-consciousness and the democratic attitude. The Central Government in India established three Academies for Arts and Letters and they are playing a very vital role in these fields, by the liberal grants to the three Academies (Sangeeta, Sahitya and Lalitkala and by the institution of National Awards to the deserving authors and artists.

The equality for opportunity enshrined in our Constitution is no doubt an egalitarian concept but due to various factors, pressures may develop within a political system towards uniformity. While in a democratic system this kind of egalitarianism has its own value, the democratic method should not kill or dampen the basic urges for self-expression, for each citizen has different aspects and does not need or accept what is given to him as the best. The doctrine that each man has certain fundamental rights guaranteed in a written Constitution as we have in India, sets a limitation within the social structure. Therefore, social planning in a democracy has to come in a peaceful way. Only then it is possible to have the continued loyalty of the people to the Constitution. Freedom variety, congenial climate for self-expression and a national consciousness—all these things should be kept open. This represents the core of the Indian culture from the millenium of years past. Inspite of obvious differences in this sub-continent, it has been possible for India to live as a single unit in the past only because of these underlying characteristics in the traits of the country.

But in the economic sphere, the position is slightly different. The Plan has emphatically expressed the urgency to remedy the inequalities of wealth and opportunity for employment and living. Time is of the great urgency, and people look to the Indian leaders with a hope that their poverty can be remedied and all arrears of progress will be attended to. In this context, the strategy of planning has to be worked out for survival of democracy in India.

—:—

III

THE GREAT EXPERIMENT OF PLANNING

The democratic political method which Nehru had ushered in aimed at socio and economic planning and brought to the surface the democratic virtues of freedom, variety, self-consciousness and a sane awareness of human fallibility and nationalism. These attributes represented the underlying characteristics of Indian culture from the millions of years in the past. Inspite of obvious differences in the sub-continent, Nehru laid down it would be possible to live as a single national unity only because of these characteristics in the traits of the country and the people inhabiting it. If Nehru had discovered that the people of India belonged to a rich heritage and this underlying current of unity bound the Indian-masses to a sense of mental tolerance, to an awareness of oneness, he thought they should have been chosen by God to fulfil a noble purpose of life in the years to come. This sense of awareness was, in fact, the greatest discovery of Nehru and he gave it a new turn and a new direction in the purpose of the Indian life. The political misfortunes were over. India had become free. The whole world was reconstructing its environments after the great destruction of the Second War. The people abroad were articulating a highly sophisticated society and making life more meaningful. Nehru realised in all his various doings that vital energy was visible everywhere even in remote villages from the highest to the lowest, that vital energy which was now freed from foreign domination and would create new fields of activity and open new avenues for gainful operation. The leaders of India had created a number of institutions to blend the apparently divirsified elements in the Indian society into a single fabric of nationalism. They had achieved the widest measure of tolerance and compressed all the differences into a harmonious whole and evolved a new class that was emerging out in the post-Republican era.

What will be the objectives of the new class? Are they going to stagnate or hold themselves up to a loftier purpose, or are they going to be desolate and again confine themselves to a period of mental slavery and physical inertia? The wolves of insecurity were present both in the Indian soil and on the Indian borders. These wolves were no more than the forces that break the institutions which Gandhi, Patel and Nehru had laboured to build them up. When Gandhi laid stress on the purity of methods, Nehru laboured for the loftiness of his objectives. When the national policy was built up, Nehru was slowly giving it an international colour so that these two ideals became not only the foundations of the Indian fabric but also the bulwark for the code of his international and foreign policy. The ease with which he worked on these ideals during the period of transition of India from foreign domination to a period of consolidation and reform must surely be attributed to the personal leadership of Mr. Nehru. Even elder statesmen like Patel, Rajenbabu and C. R. had acquisced in his leadership and they were pulling on shoulder to shoulder as comrades and worked with him for one purpose On his part Nehru treated all these elderly gentlemen with respect and got in return their loyalty and goodwill.

The planning method pursued by the Indian Planning Commission was conspicuously the greatest gift of Mr. Nehru to the posterity of India. Upon the Planning Commission fell the burden of planning for economic democracy the ideals of which had been enshrined in the Constitution. For the first time in the world planning came to be used as an instrument for moulding in an integrated way the nation's manifold activities. The Indian planning method differs from the Soviet planning in that we function under a democratic set-up which we have deliberately adopted and enshrined in our Constitution and in the Parliament. The Planning Commission has no right to draft any kind of plan which has no realtion to our Constitution or to the federal set-up of the country. With this in-built limitation and the democratic function of the allied institutions, planning has been used as a new experiment which galvanised the top leaders, administrators and the people at large into a planned effort to self-amelioration. The draft outline of the plan received the joint approval of Parliament and underwent changes in the light of criticism by all parties of the country. While the changes in the content of the plan were real we did not swerve from certain ideals or objectives which we held to us fast.

The Industrial Revolution which the West had witnessed in the early 19th century and the Soviet Union in the first quarter of the 20tn century, brought changes and many lessons from which we learned that India must be industrialised as rapidly as possible. Industrialisation included all kinds of industries, major, middling, small, village and cottage. The central objective of planning in India as stated by the Planning Commission was that planning must aim not only to raise the standard of living of the people but also to open to them avenues for a richer and a more varied life. In other words, planning must aim both at utilising more effectively the resources—human and material—available to the community so as to obtain from them not only a larger output of goods and services but also at reducing inequalities of income, wealth and *opportunity*. The programme aiming only at raising output might result in increased wealth flowing into the hands of a few leaving the mass of people in their present state of poverty. It would thus fail to achieve the wider social objectives. It was emphasised that the State would have to play a crucial role in the implementation of the goals of the plan. This involved a progressive widening of t e Public Sector and the re-orientation of the Private Sector to suit the needs of a planned economy.

The Indian plan was also an attempt to integrate the agricultural, industrial, social, economic and other aspects of the country into a single framework of thinking. An integrated plan for the economic growth of the country for greater mobilisation of resources had to be drawn up within the framework of political democracy. This method of peaceful progress and the method of democrtatic progress took care of the core of the conflict in the society and the strains involved and aimed to remove the cravings of the individual in all spheres. The plan was not merely one of setting up a few factories here or there or an increasing production in selected fields like industry and agriculture or power. There lay beneath the surface an attempt to gradually develop the infra-structure of society whose ways of thinking and action had been fossilised in the centuries before into a dead-wood of inaction and inertia. Nehru realised that a plan should aim at bringing out that dynamic quality, that quality of vision and that revolutionary quality which even our experts might lack in many spheres. This kind of planning helped us in having an emotional awareness of our problems as a whole. It brought within the fold of the framework of the plan the isolated problems of villages and districts and the remote States and areas of the country. It helped industries by tariffs and other kinds of regulation and gave many a sense of use in the scheme of planners for the benefit of the unemployed millions. The three plans contained the essence of development in the infra-structure of the society. It dealt with the Private and the Public Sector of the country. For the first time, the Private Sector came to be regulated as a controlled sector. The emergence of a mixed economy was the direct result of the planning effort. The control over the Private Sector related not only to its dividends and profits but extended to all strategic points in the economy of the country like the allocation of foreign exchange, import of raw-materials, employment of technicians and approval of foreign collaboration, agreements etc. Even banking and insurance which lay largely in the Private Sector came to be controlled by Government. The regulation of certain basic and key industries also received consideration in the Plan. The essential basis for development of industry, namely, electricity , was not neglected. This plan was not merely quantitative aiming at the physical targets; the content of the plan and the methods pursued have become far more important than the quantitative objectives for their achievements. In short, the re-making of India on the basis of democratic planning rested on the main crest, namely, the utilisation of our resources—men and material —and in particular the maximum quality and quantity of labour willingly given and rightly directed so as to promote the good of the community and of the individual. The foundations of a sound planning were laid on the realities of the day in bringing about a new social order free from exploitation. As Nehru himself pointed out it was a set-up towards the establishment of a society which gave security to individuals and offered employment and encouragement to creative activity and adventure.

This concept of planning to be translated into action required a series of administrative steps from the top to the bottom. It travelled to the frontiers of the States, territories, District Boards and Municipal Councils. For the first time in the country, the community scheme was initiated so that millions of people came to be aware of the grand planning effort that has been taking place at all levels of administration. What was the community scheme intended to do ? Something like the social engineering of the village as a whole; a sum total of all additional food grown, schools and dispensaries, better roads, tanks, wells etc. In fact, under this scheme of planning, the object created would not be so important as the feeling that the villager himself whether he is qualified or not, was participating in the great experiment. In the true sense the villager got trained to the problem of community-living and adapted himself to that kind of work for building up the integrated village and community life of the country. In other words, the villager became not only the builder of his own village centre but also of India as a whole.

This kind of re-building of India was a novel concept in that planning and execution were pushed down from the top administrator to the level of the village workers.... There are too many backward areas in the country to which the spear-head of the planning activity may not percolate. To such sectors of backwardness the planning effort is taken straight to the lowest level with a view to make the village workers gain a wealth of experience of various types of work and the various conditions and build within themselves a sense of leadership.

Within a few weeks after he became the Vice-President of the interim Government on September 2, 1946, Nehru took all steps which were to prove very important later. The first was the appointment of an Advisory Planning Board which recommended the setting-up of the Planning Commission. The other was the constitution of the Scientific Man-Power Committee which laid the foundations for rapid technical advance and technical education and the setting up of a chain of National Laboratories. Nehru felt that while foreign capital and foreign technical know-how was necessary, this inflow of technical knowledge and the corresponding training of Indians in new fields of production would be desirable. Technology in India had to be oriented with reference to the needs of the situation. In agriculture and village and small-scale industries, where the employment potential is vast and unlimited, power could be used as a source of energy and the hand-driven appliances could be converted into mechanical propulsions. With this idea the Ambar Charkha was introduced to replace the hand-driven charkha a few years ago and the substitution of power looms for hand-driven looms was on instance in this direction. This method not only retained the trade for the family but also improved the economic resources by augmenting its daily income in the shape of higher productivity. The avenues and development of power were an innovation by which India benefitted in the planning periods unlike Britain which started its industrial career some three hundred years ago on coal-based energy but which proved weaker on account of the competition by later entrants like the U.S.S.R., Germany, the U.S.A. etc. Even during the days of conversion from coal to power Britain experienced a number of difficulties and its present high-cost structure is perhaps due to these difficulties persisting in some of her own industries.

During the last 30 years there has been tremendous growth in U.S.S.R. in the fields of agriculture and manufacture. This enormous development was rendered possible because of the over-emphasis of the Soviet education system in science and technology. The conclusions reached by the high-powered Technical Committee which submitted its report to the President of the U.S.A. soon after the launching of the spaceship by the U.S.S.R. very much ahead of the U.S.A., reaffirmed the superiority of the Russian technical system of education and the top advisers in the U.S.A. Administration have made recommendations for a re-orientation in scientific and technological educational policies. They have begun to wonder that inspite of enormous expenditure and the huge army of personnel employed, the U.S.A. could not keep pace with the U.S.S.R. in certain fields. If this challenge of technical superiority is re-affirmed by further achievements in a conspicuous way by the U.S.S.R., many American Administrators would begin to wonder whether any change in their existing planning method would be necessary within their democratic set-up. In other words, from the point of view of technique, the U.S.A. is interested that the experiment conducted in India of *planning* with *democracy* should succeed over the strategies of the popular form of Government. They should themselves feel eager to see that a democratic planning adopted by India should succeed at any cost and should pose a serious challenge to the methods pursued by the Communist form of planning and implementation.

The slowly diminishing tension and the fading out of the clouds of cold war weakened the basis of military blocks and each advanced nation in the West realising its more fortunate position began to give as friendly gestures and as sacrifices, and to make generous offers of equipment and technical knowledge for the advancement of India's material prosperity. The ideals of peace and international friendship which were laid on the foundations of disarmament and nuclear ban, brought for India goodwill and understanding both in the fields of international cooperation and trade and commerce and industrial development. Nehru strengthened the Ambassadorial ties and set up a number of missions in distant countries and he sent men of culture as our Ambassadors abroad. This foreign policy began to yield rich dividends in the years to come in the fields of trade and commeree, technical assistance, culture and education and also in the larger field of international co operation and unity.

In the context of the special requirements of the planned effort, enlightened nations of the West came out of their own voluntary efforts to give sizable offers of help to a sizable portion of the world's population inhabiting the Indian sub continent. Never before in the history of the world did the nations come so close to one another as now as a result of the advancements made by science and technology. India was thus fortunate in embarking on her industrial career not only by the exchange of expert advice and the give and take in economic and monetary fields but also by the availability on easy terms of technical assistance and capital aid. She also reaped the fruits of rising technology and advancement in the means of production and thereby reduced the period of gestation by discriminating choice of association and participation of the giver country. The blessings of knowledge were thus tamed and harnessed to the material prosperity of India.

India, while standing for the progress and freedom for *all* nations, recognised the diversity in the patterns of ideologies and administrations in the world and in this climate she built her mutual goodwill and tolerance on these diverse patterns. The fact that we were trying to solve the problem of human want by well-recognised democratic methods added to the world's esteem of India and appreciation of her efforts. This policy of winning friendship and well-wishers in foreign lands had created doubts during the initial period of our foreign policy in the efficacy of the methods pursued but in the long rnn a nation comes to be judged by its moral principles and its experiments with those principles in actual performance. Therefore, at times, our foreign policy had imposed heavy stresses and strains but in the long years of events that soon followed, the nation was able to forge a happy and harmonious relationship with all the supplying countries by its own exemplary conduct in her international policies.

Coming to the internal policies, India had borne its stresses and strains with a certain amount of fortitude. We tried our utmost to collect our resources and depend upon foreign aid only to the extent it was necessary and in certain wanted fields. Austerity measures curbing conspicuous consumption were resorted to and a heavy tax effort was the prelude to a request for foreign aid on a massive scale. All our countrymen whether in towns or in the contry-side, were asked to ponder over the situation and make their share of the sacrifice for the building of India. Aid was accepted from almost all the advanced countries without strings and on a policy of utilising it in a manner that was suited to the Indian economy as well as to the giver country. Repayment of debt obligations was scrupulously adhered to although it involved heavy stresses and strains in our uncomfortable period of foreign exchange shortage.

In the ideal of planning the means were given

undue importance. Toil at home and acceptance of aid without strings while sticking to the principles of peace and co-existence were the cardinal features of the internal and external policies of India. Means were regarded as important as the ends and both constituted the summum bonum of all human efforts. It may be said that if any of man's achievements threatens to destroy the end itself human society must take cognisance of it and make every effort to avert such a catastrophe. Every thinking Indian, nay, the citizen of the world, has, therefore, a right not only to advert to this important question but also to live by it as far as he can.

In the Nehru era of economic planning two important developments of immense and incalculable dimensions for humanity had taken place. One was the tremendous advance in science and technology resulting in the development of nuclear energy and the conquest of space throwing wide open unlimited vista of progress *or* destruction. Indin preferred the path of peace and was willing to let her neighbours help her for constructive purposes. On this basis we accepted a policy of atomic power development and refused to become a nuclear power of weapons. The other was an important phenomenon of a different type which related not so much to material development as to the growing awakening and an almost irresistible move of the long-suppressed masses of humanity in the continents, particularly in Asia and Africa, which had like India been submerged in the slavery of ignorance and superstition. Both these totally different, but not necessarily antagonistic, expressions of elemental energy were capable of infinite good as well as of infinite evil. We members of Asia had a common culture and our memory goes back into long depths of time. This insistence of our heritage which sprang from the meditations of the wisest men in the distant past was the core of our friendship between the Eastern and Southern neighbours. For, a culture, like life, is a growing, living thing and any change in the spirit of our national life of the country begins to reflect at once the character of its culture. It is true that this tolerant approach to problems tempered with the marked ethical quality of our past is bound to influence the vital elements of our identity and unity. Therefore, in our efforts in industrialising and changing the face of the country we always kept in mind the artistic expression, thus blending our traditional spirit of humality and co-operation with sympathetic understanding and goodwill. This synthesis of old and new, this kind of a survival and progress without conflict and tension is perhaps the greatest gift of Nehru. The roots of Indian unity were drawing sustenance from a common faith in certain ideas, ideals of human existence in spite of diverse patterns of differences based on region, religion, varieties of languages,varying levels of development of culture, literature and arts. Animated with this spirit we helped our neighbours like Burma, Nepal, Sikkim, Ceylon and some of the African countries. Even our trade channels with Pakistan were re-opened and we sent goodwill missions to that country. This feeling of tolerance for the views of others had diminished the fears of cold war and reduced the tensions. This formula of progress on the basis of co-existence came to be accepted as an active faith by both the Western and American and the Russian Blocs. In this mighty task the integration of mind and hearts and over a period of 17 years and over a vast stretch of territory emanated as the single unmixed blessing of the Prime Minister's peace policy in the last 50's and 60's. The message of discipline and exhortations to the Indians living abroad from time to time by the visiting President and the Prime Minister re-affirmed India's good intentions and the roles of unity and universality of culture were strengthened.

—o—

IV

THE GRAND TRANSFORMATION

When Nehru assumed leadership of the country and the Party and tried to implement some of the objectives laid down in the Constitution, he had certain difficulties to start with. The economic policy of the Government and the Party had to be very precisely defined with a view to disabuse the minds of foreign investors of certain wrong impressions that had come to prevail in the minds of foreign investors in the country and abroad. The Government also had to evolve a working policy to a goal which they had set before themselves both at the Party level and in the Centre and the States, and this policy got reiteration in the election manifesto and at various meetings of the AICC held at different places. The Resolution on Industry passed at Ajmer at one of the sessions of the AICC should appear to be a very clear and forthright and comprehensive statement of Government's working policy. The amplification and the emphasis that the Resolution sought to make was made in the speech of the Congress President and the Prime Minister, Pt. Jawaharlal Nehru. The same policy underwent a further change at the Avadi meeting held in 1954. Earlier, the Kalyani Session of the Congress Party had also laid the foundations of the industrial development of modern India. The Prime Minister made frequent utterances on economic and industrial policy of Government at various meetings of the National Development Council and in the Parliament, and in his various speeches in the country and abroad. While the objective was clear the approach had to be entirely pragmatic because the institutions for implementing the objectives were still to be *evolved* and a coherent working policy adopted for translation into action. The main difficulty in the pragmatic approach was that there was a constant change in the forces in the country as well as abroad and the technological world was undergoing a rapid change due to the invention of nuclear power. In this context, there was not only a need for a change in the tools that were to be used for industrial development but also in the change of patterns of our own thinking. The uncertainties created as a result of the mutual relationship among the big powers in the world and the emergence of China as a potential nuclear power on the borders of northern India and a militarily armed belligerent Pakistan had also given a re-orientation to the thinking of the industrial and economic policies of the Government.

The Encyclopaedia of Social Sciences begins its article on 'Socialism' as follows :—

"The terms socialism, communism and collectivism which are found to be used interchangeably are ambiguous and ill-defined. For this reason they have an exceedingly wide range of specific connotations."

Therefore, one of the difficulties in understanding the socialistic pattern of state as propounded by Prime Minister Nehru was to give a content to that word; the content which meant different things at different times, different things to different groups and also different things to different individuals. The history of socialism throughout the ages has shown that there have been many facets to it : some being largely emotional and humanitarian in content, woven with religious fervour, others with specific economic and political objectives. Even Marxian socialism undoubtedly gave it a certain amount of dynamism but in the process of making it dynamic and virile it evoked the resistance of a large body of socialists mainly because of its ruthlessness. Since the emergence of Marx, socialism proper has taken various shapes in different countries.

The intellectuals in India were also affected in varying degrees by the socialistic ideas and concepts. Therefore, when the Congress 'rebels' assumed the role of responsibility for ameliorating the sufferings of the Indian masses, they took upon themselves with a great amount of sympathy a role that existed between the Fabians of England, and later between the British Labour Party and the Indian politicians. Therefore, if consciously or unconsciously any objection was raised to the socialistic objectives of Nehru's Government either by Indian capitalists or by foreign investors it amounted to objection to the very basis on which the Congress organisation, and later the Indian leaders *forming* part of that Congress organisation, was based. The Congress Party, symbolising the aspirations of the suffering millions, came still to be regarded as a National Government and it drew its strength from the vast majority of the Indian people. The mere fact that there were other parties in the country, did not detract from the socialistic content of the Congress policy. The famous resolution of the Karachi Congress of 1931 laid down more or less the broad principles on which the Constitution of India had been framed. The Karachi Resolution as amended by the AICC in Bombay in August, 1931, stated—"*inter alia*', a State shall own or control key industries and services, mineral resources, railways, water-ways, shipping and other means of public transport." The resolution passed at the AICC session in Ajmer later echoed the central core of the scheme. Therefore, when the country was ripe for adoption of the socialistic patterm of State in 1954, there was no surprise at all because the purpose behind the Congress Government had been clearly stated earlier on very many occasions.

There was also a need for making a distinction between a socialistic welfare state and the economic welfare of a country. Social welfare which should be the main objective of a welfare state has been described by Simon Kuznets as the positive element in the satisfaction of man's wants, men viewed as members of society and he distinguished this from economic welfare by quoting Prof. Pigou, that is, economic welfare means that part of social welfare that can be brought directly or indirectly into relation with the measuring rod of money. The elements entering into the consideration of economic welfare and social welfare are more complex, for the question is not merely one of deciding between economic progress and social welfare but also of determining whether *desirable* and *necessary* social reform should precede or be deferred until there has been sufficient economic advance. In a changing world like ours new conditions and new forces appear and an indiscriminate preference for economic growth and postponement of certain *social* changes would result in incalculable consequences in the future and the adoption of a working policy in the framework of a Parliamentary Democracy would appear to be very difficult. In an under-developed country, especially like India, the important limiting factors are time (that is, how soon the objective is proposed to be achieved), resources (physical and financial), a clear thinking on the objectives of planned development (that is, decisions regarding allocation of resources between consumption and investment, changes in social structure and scheme of resource mobilisation etc.). It also involves a basic decision on the economic growth combined with stipulations regarding the pattern of development that should take place in various sectors of the economy such as agricultural development, expansion of heavy and basic industries, defence requirements, employment opportunities and also the shifting character of emphasis at various times.

The several steps taken by the Central Government and by the State governments since 1947 pieced together would undoubtedly indicate that the Government's objective was towards providing greater satisfaction of the wants of the citizens of India than what obtained in the period prior to Independence. Some schemes like D.V.C. or Bhakra Nangal, yield results in a limited period of time and the effect of such schemes can be only felt and cannot be measured in terms of economic cost as they have a welfare content. Eugene Stately in his book "Future of Under-Developed Countries" stated the following on India :

"............In India, the responsibilities of independence seem to have given added impetus to the will to develop. Here is a case most important in the under-developed world where an enlightened political leadership which believes strongly in democratic values is striving with great intellegence, but in the face of tremendous handicaps, to *lead* not *drive* the people towards a better future."

He also states, "There are plenty of unwise Government attitudes and regulations which tend to smother constructive business initiative, but the real task is much more positive. It is a task of institution building. Just as under-developed countries have under-development Governments, they also have under-developed private business communities. There is a lack of real business enterprise, business know-how and business integrity and a sense of social responsibility. For private enterprise to make the contribution it should, in this country, personnel must be developed by training and experience, organisations must be established and philosophies must change. This last implies changes in every aspect of a country's social system." The above quotations had no great bearing on Indian Government's economic and industrial policies but it helps one to understand the nature and content of private enterprise in under-developed countries; even more valuable is the emphasis on Government's initiative and the need for institutional building and growth. No doubt the objectives of the Government were socialistic and the means of production should both serve to contribute to the welfare of the people by raising the standard of living of the individual and, in the larger perspective, the country's economic progress.

Even at the outset it would be necessary to avoid any mis-conception arising out of the political and economic implications of the objectives. The concept of the State intervening in the economic life of the individual is not peculiar to India alone as even some of the advanced capitalistic countries believe in tempering concentration of wealth for the purpose of maintaining healthy competition. Therefore, for India, it is not a question of believing in the efficacy of the market forces but also a recognition of the fact that the very large area over which the market forces have to operate neutralises its influence for the good of the community. It would be also idle to talk of any possible prospect of a "counterveiling power", operating as a counterveiling factor against concentration of economic power in a country like India arising. Therefore, the path of the Indian Government was very clear when they enunciated the principle of the 'mixed economy', that is, the concept of State-controlled enterprises in partnership with private enterprise. In this field there existed also an area of small-scale industries where the workers had to be helped in a number of ways and required protection against undue pressure that would be exerted on him by the "old and new market forces" to maintain himself as a self-reliant entity in the fields in which he was working.

In the context of the growing functions of the State, political considerations apart, there was also a need for re-defining the relationship and the area and scope of co-operation of the various sectors in the economy for the purpose of attaining the common objectives of the socialistic State. With an industrial system that was inherited dynasticism in private enterprise had not much scope in the future. The essential feature of a private enterprise in a democratic socialistic State is that it permits a persoinwho is at the bottom of the scale to rise tothe top position if he has the ability to do so. Therefore, in a democratic State like India where political opportunities for individual citizens have been afforded on Constitutional foundations, a society that was still to be evolved in the economic sphere has also to recognise the need for allowing talent to develop and take its own appropriate place in those sectors of society where talent and leadership are essential. Prof. Rostow, in his book on the process of economic growth has something pertinent to say both in regard to the role of Government in industrialisation and the switching over of the elite from private enterprise to Government institutions. He says :

"Once the institutions of Government responsibility and action are in motion it becomes increasingly difficult for private investment to operate in the old way. In such a setting young men of vigour attracted by the excitement and risks of the most responsible positions, turn increasingly to the institutions where such decisions are taken; and these institutions are now more likely to be the Departments of Governments than the offices of business and industrial firms."

It is no doubt difficult to define precisely the frontiers of Government control and private initiative. If an effort is to be made to make an economy self-reliant, a great deal of development would have to take place not only in the private sector but also in such fields where the private sector is not adequately represented because of various limitations. The filling up of all this gap by Governmental action and institution is not only a matter of expediency but also an urgent necessity. In his book on Government's role in economic life, Prof. Steiner has defined this adjustment of Governmental function fully; he says :

"This channelised function of Government can be narrowed a bit to focus attention upon the broad relationship between Government and the economic order. Thus,

(1) Government is the principal social institution through which man can make decisions about the goals and methods of economic system ;

(2) Government exercises its power to ensure adherence to the goals and methods; and,

(3) Government protects individuals from coercions within and without society that conflict with or jeopardize the attainment of common goals and the proper use of the methods."

If these premises are accepted as a basis to guide the acceptance of Government's interference by the people concerned and by others who deal with such a Government, the problems can be recognised in proper perspective. Again, to borrow the idea from Prof. Steiner,

"What is necessary particularly in the case of the industrialisation of an economy like India's where a certain amount of development has already taken place, is to attempt a symmetrical view of the problems of Government control." He says, "This symmetrical view demands that any analysis of the expanding economic power assumed by Government would be incomplete and one-sided unless the expanding powers of various types of economic institutions already existing and likely to develop are considered in relation to it. The tendency towards expansion of State functions in this field might look overpowering unless one takes a symmetrical view of economic activity."

If in this context the leaders of the Government as well as the captains of private industry are inclined to subordinate their proclivities to the needs of building up a symmetrical structure, the character of conflict within India may change and many problems may not arise. But as it does, in the process of filling up the gaps where the initiative largely rests upon Government, it might be that Governmental activity is greater in proportion than the activity of the private sector. The future of the Indian economy requires a day-to-day reconciliation of its relationship; but it is only a matter of detail. For the overall objective of the country as a whole rapid industrialisation and increasing Government interference in the industrialisation of the country is a harsh imperative.

The future adjustment of relationship will no doubt arise out of several considerations. For instance, concentration of Government initiative will have to be made on the producer goods industries because these industries demand a heavier outlay of capital and control over complementary and ancillary products which cannot be achieved unless production is either in Government sphere or it is carried on in close co-operation with Government. The field open for the private sector is still vast, especially for a country of the size of India and a market of the people inhabiting the territory of the Indian sub-continent. It could be asked no doubt that the cream of profitable enterprises would be taken up by the State Government leaving the unimportant ones to private enterprise. But by and large in the producer goods industry where the gestation period is long, consumers' propensity, either dictated by a desire to expand his needs or determined by his ability to buy, does not operate directly. Therefore, the price factor in the case of producer goods industry carries a certain amount of resilience with it. So long as Government is in control of the economic machine and can regulate imports and also licence the starting of industries and also reach the industrialist through a properly attenuated taxation system, there is no need to assume that private industry would act detrimentally to Government's interest. Subject to the availability of resources and employment opportunities there should be a full utilisation opportunity by the Government as well as the Private Sector, the emphasis being on the production of all those parts which can be economically produced.

The concept of democratic socialism is peculiarly Nehru's gift to India. It is born out of India's genius and it is essentially an intellectual concept. The democratic aspect of it compels leaders to lead and not drive. The socialistic aspect carries with it a large element of control, regulation and regimentation and planning. The determination of how much leadership has to be provided and how much regulation is necessarily a matter of pragmatic approach to be forged into the economic structure without impairing the democratic foundations. Even for such democratic functioning it should be realised goals have to be fixed, methods have to be determined and both have to be pursued. The task is a very difficult one because it is easy to speak a language of capitalism; it is even more easy to speak the language of those who believe in an all-powerful State, but those who believe in democratic socialism can only say what the contents and objectives are and this is what the citizens of India want—a peculiar combination of humanism and progress.

The adoption by Parliament in December, 1954, of the socialistic pattern of society as the objective of the social and economic development required that all industries of basic and strategic importance or in the nature of public utility services should be under the ownership and control of the Public Sector. Thus, the State was slowly persuaded to assume more responsibility for industrial development over a wider area than before. When we came to the end of the first five-year period of the Plan, the country was already producing new items like acetate rayon, staple fibre, some important heavy chemicals like calcium carbide, hydrogen peroxide etc., a number of dyes, diesel engines, locomotives and automobile components. The country was in a mood to embark on a bolder programme of production at the beginning of the Second Plan. The Industrial Policy Resolution of 1956 and the amendment of Article 31 and 31 (A) of the Constitution and the enforcement of the Companies Act and the report of the Taxation Enquiry Commission had created doubts as to the ultimate purpose of the State interference in the field of industry. Time and again, various pronouncements had been made that the field open to the Private Sector was enormous, and all that Government wanted to do was in the nature of filling up the gap with a view to achieve a particular level of production and fulfilling social obligations. Planning with regard to key industries was becoming more and more a positive concept and Government was interested to see that the Private Sector served the social purpose while it received all help from Government. The economic concentration of wealth and power in a few hands was slowly becoming a menace with which Government had to contend with and the surest remedy was not only greater production of wealth but also equitable distribution through State participation. Even countries without any socialist bias were increasingly taking responsibilities towards their poor citizens who by Indian standards could be considered to be quite well off. In a country like the U.K. the Governments, whether Labour or Conservative, have followed policies ofnationalisation of some of the key industries and some policies which have falsified the Marxian philosophy of the proletarianism of the middle class. We, in India, were far, far away from the standard of living of the people of the middle class of that country, yet we were working towards the same objective, namely, the raising of incomes all round and reducing disparities.

Apart from this wider social purpose, the severe limitations on our resources and the ambitious nature of our planning required that there should be a careful husbanding of our resources and that these limited resources were canalised into essential industries for national development. The idea of such overall regulation of economic activities is inherent in any planned effort. Even during war time such control had existed and now when the war against poverty has just started the Private Sector must accept regulation by the State.

When the Planning Commission was to be constituted in 1950 the draft of the resolution setting out the terms of reference for the Planning Commission came up for consideration. Shri Nehru re-wrote a considerable part of the draft and in particular he linked up the work of the Planning Commission directly with the Fundamental Rights and to the Directive Principles of State Policy embodied in the Constitution. The idea was that he rooted India's planning effort in the twin concept of democracy and socialism with a view to provide equal opportunity and a good life to the masses of the people. At the meeting of the National Development Council on November 9, 1954 he stated, "I am not using the words 'a socialistic picture of society in a dogmatic sense but in the sense of meaning largely that the means of production should be socially owned and controlled for the benefit of the society as a whole." The dominance of private enterprise throughout the world had become out of date and any system based on the acquisitiveness of the society was not only absolutely out of date but also *immoral*. The urges of the people pointed out the necessity for going in that direction and he believed in our capacity to win them rather than fight them. He said, "We can bring about social changes and development under pressure of events, by the pressure of democracy and also by friendly cooperative approach rather than an approach of trying to eliminate each other and the stronger party winning. I think we can do "that even in the industrial field."

Nehru did not wish to nationalise and waste resources in compensating private parties but certain fields of activity should be sacrosanct for the State and the Public Sector should be given a greater scope. There should be a greater stress on heavy machine making industry as that was to be the basis of industrial growth. The approach to industrial development as laid down in the policy of 1956 was applied successively to steel, coal and oil, in each case after a degree of controversy. In steel and oil in particular, without the strong personal support of Mr. Nehru it would have been difficult to proceed very far. These trends were helped by what was at that time a new factor in India's development, namely, an offer of economic and technical aid by the Soviet Union. The Second Plan also envisaged a substantial expansion of foreign trade with East European countries, especially the U.S.S.R. Government set up the State Trading Corporation in 1955 to canalise trade in that direction and as a measure to fill up the gap in the un-coordinated efforts of the Private Sector in the field of trade.

Nehru declared, "You must go to the root and the base and build up that root and base on which you will build up the structure of industrial growth. Therefore, it is heavy industries that count; nothing else counts, excepting as a balancing factor which is of course important. We want planning for heavy machine making industries and heavy industries. We want industries that make heavy machines and we should set about them as rapidly as possible "because it takes time." The concept of building a strong industrial base and an economy capable of self-sustained growth dominated as the main theme for the Third Plan and this concept had to be fully integrated in India s approach to other issues like technical , distributive, managerial and financial fields. Action for economic and social change in the rural areas lay largely in the States. But it was possible for a country like India so large in size and with huge population to energise the adjoining areas around the big manufacturing units for which the Private Sector would be hesitant to take steps. Ultimately, the future of India lay in bridging up the gaps in education; in the need to ensure a certain minimum of amenities to the people in the rural areas; in the solving of problems like slum clearance and slum improvement in the cities and in the welfare of the children and socially disabled and insecure, old citizens. The emphasis, therefore, in the Third Plan on these aspects of development was strongly reinforced by the views which Nehru urged repeatedly within the Planning Commission and in other forums.

Nehru realised that the costliest thing in planning was time lost to action. Therefore, when the size of the Public Sector in Third Plan was to be determined he stated that the physical programmes to be accepted for implementation over the five-year period should not be limited by the availability of financial resources immediately in sight or at the time of drawing up the plan. He advised that the programme for industrial development including power, transport, technical, educational and scientific research, should proceed in a coordinated manner in accordance with the approved scheme of priorities so that when foreign exchange and internal resources became available these things could be implemented. Whatever we could do ourselves by way of advance action or otherwise should be done.

When the objectives for planned development for the Third Plan were considered, at the request of the National Development Council, Shri Nehru took the draft to Kulu, worked upon it para by para adding substantial portions and improving upon others, and thus emerged the final statement which forms the first chapter of the Third Plan Report. In this portion he linked present development to the aspirations and outlook of leaders of our national movement, drew the economic progress and welfare of each country and fitted it into a framework of our efforts to build up a liberated humanity. He stated, "Planning is a continuous process..... Perspective planning is of the essence of the planning process. As this process develops there is a certain rhythm of expansion in the development of the people and a sense of enterprise and achievement because of them. They are conscious of a purpose in life and have a feeling of being participants in the making of history. Ultimately, it is the development of the human being and the human personality that counts. Although planning involves material investment, even more important is the investment in man. The people of India today, with all their burdens and problems, live on the frontier of a new world which they are helping to build. In order to cross this frontier they have to possess courage and enterprise, the spirit of endurance and capacity for hard work, and the vision of the future."

In the second year of the Third Plan when the

aggression by China took place came the critical moment for planning. At the height of the crisis early in November, 1962, Nehru set his face firmly against any attempt to nibble at the Plan from within. He stated, "We are at the cross-roads of history and are facing great historical problems on which depends our future." The Plan was the warp and woof of our national life and it was the war effort itself that required the Plan. The non-essentials should be kept down and the basic objectives of the Plan should be pursued in vital terms.

Planning in a federal democratic structure brings up different problems from time to time. As far back as 1951, Nehru had decided to set up a National Development Council. He stressed at every stage to achieve national consensus. He tried to seek the counsel of various political parties and other groups and get their support for the Plan. In all these actions he had set up an institution in the Planning Commission and the cooperation of the States in the National Development Council and committed these institutions to work for the national good.

In India, curiously enough, a new role has been forced upon Indian capitalism after the adoption by the Parliament of the socialistic objectives of the State. The capitalistic system in India has had an exotic origin. The businessman in India has been either a land-lord or money-lender. He did not enter into industry or trade to any large extent. It is the misfortune of Indian capitalism that it has emerged as a powerful entity at a time when it is to play a significant social purpose and when politically a large part of the world has found that this system has no vitality. In the Western countries the capitalist system has some traditions. But, unfortunately, in India in view of its comparatively recent origin, it has not established any tradition. It has not built up any body of persons or a corps to develop any tradition to fit into our economic structure consistent with our economic objectives. Even in the advanced countries like the U.S.A., the several Federal Acts against monopolist combines and cartels are indicative of the fear of economic concentration of power though State regulation of cartels and monopolies has not resulted in diminishing the political power of vested interests to any great extent. The curious position that democracy and capitalism occupy in the mind of the American public is portrayed in Galbraith's book on American Capitalism. Counterveiling power as a check on capitalism may be true of the United States, but such counterveiling factors did not exist in another country; at any rate, not in India. American capitalism is young: it has abundant natural resources and the people enjoy a high standard of living. The same may be said to be true to some extent to India. But in other countries the test by which capitalist system is justified is not so much its efficiency but whether its efficiency is in the direction of profit-making and whether it can subordinate its objectives to the social objectives of production and distribution. In India there should be several individual capitalists who run their enterprises very efficiently and that only indicates the capitalist as a manager of a very well-run unit. But some justification is necessary for the capitalist system to function during a period of transition such as that we witness in our economy at present. And that justification arises mainly because of the ability of mobilising private capital. Even this fact was challenged during discussions on the provision of the Company Law in regard to the managing agency system. In India an efficient entrepreneur is able to attract deposits from the public because there has been no Government institution which can provide a higher return and a higher investment possibility. Inspite of the changes made in the Company Law the role of the company promoter has not been ruled out and any hope of substantial private saving lies, to quote Ragnar Nurkse, "mainly in the re-investment of entrepreneureal profits and if this is encouraged would be an effective and almost automatic way of maximising the marginal saving ratio." In the present climate this source of capital formation cannot be lost sight of but if this process were to take place by *suo motu* action of the entrepreneur in a country like India there is much room left out and for this purpose the initiative will also have to come from the Government.

Even in a democratic country like India after the adoption of the socialistic pattern of society it seems reasonably certain that the Private Sector will have a very honourable place and that it cannot be done away with. The economy, if it is to have any vitality and become dynamic should adapt itself to the changes that occur in the process of its own growth or re-distribution of wealth and in this process a new class of people will emerge and they will have both wealth and power. Sometimes this power could be offset by a number of circumstances which a welfare state has to provide partly by the means of fiscal measures and such other devices, as the State may possibly think of. To turn the other side of the medal, nowhere in the world can the Private Sector function without State control or State help and State direction. The experience which led to the failure of many Indian parties in the initial period to obtain the collaboration of foreign industrialists in many new ventures profitable enough in themselves for such foreign investment, is an indication that by and large in a country like India, Private Sector cannot flourish without Governmental support. The State also has to realise that even in an egalitarian economy they will have to have an entrepreneural class to mobilise the corporate savings, and for purpose of entreprenurial ability. If planning means utilisation of all resources wisely and well and in the direction of reaching the targets and consistent with the social and economic objectives of the State, the Private Sector has a definite role in the economic development. But if it is left uncontrolled the country s resources would not be utilised to the maximum extent possible in a manner which will ensure the maximum benefit to the people. In this context, the emergence of an enlightened leadership in the business and industrialist class is not only necessary but also imperative. In an under-developed country like India the actions taken by particular Governments whether they may be socialistic in character or have a pronounced bias towards untramelled private enterprise are largely dictated by the prevailing socio-economic considerations ruling from time to time. To quote Ragnar Nurkse again, in his essay on capital formation he says, "We have reached a field of sociological rather than economic consideration...That we have come to it is not surprising for the advancement of the backward countries far more than an economic problem. Even the social heritage in India does not provide favourable atmosphere for the development of capitalism. If the capitalists in India move with the times and adapt themselves to the sociological and economic changes of the country they would contribute to the smooth running of their own system and to the planning efforts of the Government.

V

THE INDUSTRIAL AND ECONOMIC ADMINISTRATION

"Destiny has cast a certain role on this country. Whether any one of us present here can be called men or women of destiny or not, I do not know. That is a big word which does not apply to average human beings, but whether we are men or women of destiny or not, *India*, is a country of destiny and so far as we represent this great country with a great destiny spread out in front of her, we also have to act as men and women of destiny viewing all our problems in that long perspective of destiny and of the world and of Asia, never forgetting the great responsibility that *freedom*, that *this great destiny* of our country has cast upon us, not losing ourselves in petty controversies and debates which might be useful but which would, in this context, be either out of place or out of tune."

(Nehru—November 8, 1948, on the Draft Constitution as framed by the Drafting Committee.)

The pioneering effort in the early 20's towards the industrial development of the country was the report of the Indian Industrial Commission in 1918 to investigate the industrial potentialities of the country. It was presided over by Sir Thomas Holland. In his famous dissenting minute in this report, Pt. Madan Mohan Malaviya expounded with more clarity the need for industrialisation and gave a national touch to it. But nothing tangible was done on this report. In 1923, Government announced the policy of discriminating protection which did not satisfy the aspirations of the county. The Bombay Plan was also a herioc attempt to put down the aspirations of the Indians but it cannot be regarded as a blue-print. Soon after independence, the country was no doubt in a mood for rapid industrialisation but economic conditions were unsuitable as a result of a number of factors such as the Korean War, the effects of partition and refugee problem and, lastly, on account of devaluation of the Rupee. Major industries like jute and tea faced crisis; the country's balance of trade and payments gave anxiety to Government on account of large-scale import of foodgrains, raw cotton, and raw jute. The partition also had created an imbalance in the economic structure of the country. The Indian Government in the post-independence period also had to face the problem of reconciling three antagonistic objectives, namely, the Commonwealth preference, the closer tie-up with other industrial countries and protection to domestic manufactures. India had been party to Sterling area arrangement and this made her foreign trade less flexible than otherwise. When India became a member of the GATT, the GATT frowned on all import restrictions except as a means of stabilising the balance of payments. In 1955, however, Indian representative in GATT was able to get the consent of the contracting parties to use quota restriction for developing their nascent industries. This could, perhaps, be regarded as the foundation-stone for international recognition for industrial development by the newly emancipated countries. Even then the country was impatient at the slow pace of development and wanted a systematic assessment of the need for expansion of the existing industries as well as the development of the potentialities of those industries for which the country was still dependent on imports. This led to the Government taking steps to foster large-scale industries. They had also to pay attention to the employment potentials of the small-scale and village industries. Thus, slowly and imperceptively, an integrated industrial development programme was in the process of formulation and the commercial policy of the Government had to be geared to suit the needs of the industrial policy.

At this time of history in India, the foreigners dominated in industry, trade and commerce exchange banks and in the general insurance field. In shipping also the bnlk of over-seas shipping business was in the hands of the foreigners. This was due largely from the fact that Indian shipping companies have not made much progress. As a result of lack of shipping facilities Indian trade has suffered very much particularly in South East Asia and Middle East where we were losing considerable amount of business. Ceylon tea has a grip over the Australian market minly because Ceylon could ship tea to Australia almost every week while it is difficult to get a ship to Australia from the eastern parts of India once a month. Great damage has also been done to our trade as the agents of foreign steam ship companies were our exporters and as exporters they were competitors to

Indian interests. While shipping freights were determined at the international level such determination was always loaded against the interests of Indian trade. Often times steamer freights between Calcutta and Rangoon and Madras and Rangoon compare unfavourably with the steamer freights from Tilbury to Rangoon. This kind of discriminatory freight structure had ruined India's export trade and this was due to lack of shipping facilities. In the matter of import business, the import control measures had changed the character of the trade and more Indian companies came to find a place than before. Even here some of the European countries began to appoint their own distributive systems and divert their business into the hands of foreign companies in India. In regard to export business the strangle-hold of foreigners had been much stronger. There were about four firms which commanded about a third of the trade in export of oils and oil seeds. Tea, jute and hides and skins are still dominated by foreign interests. Since India has no monopoly in the foreign markets of the commodities exported, we cannot attempt to make changes for a very long period. Even in the distributive trade there is a pronounced tendency for the manufacturing concerns to have their own distributive agencies and foreign interests handle this business through a subsidiary in India and get from the Indian market a price that it can bear irrespective of the cost of the article and allocate the profit so earned between the Indian company and the foreign company in the most advantageous manner to them. In the post-war period the distribution of fertilizers was taken out from one foreign concern which was operating on a monopoly basis and this resulted in the high price and faulty distribution. The above description will show that any pronouncement of Industrial policy has vital implications for the foreign interests in India.

There are certain peculiar features in the Indian economy which operate as deterrent forces to any kind of regulation or control. The country's size is so vast and the geographical distribution of industries is so poor that unless the country is equipped with an efficient transport system and distributive machinery for enforcing regulation orders, the full impact of such regulation is difficult to be felt. A large portion of important industries is still in the hands of managing agents who continue on a dynastic basis. There has been no effort to develop in the private sector an organisation of managerial development. A large portion of the Indian economy is outside the monetary side, and all monetary controls have only a partial application. The capital market in the country with a number of independent institutions, some regulated and some unregulated by law, is not integrated and private money-lenders and 'hundis' operate outside the orbit of banking regulations. Even a sizable portion of the seasonal requirements comes outside the monetary side. The Indian industries by and large have to depend upon Government institutions for equity finance. The bank rate and the stock exchange rate has no universal application. Agriculture still continues to be the occupation of sixty per cent of the people and its impact on the national economy and industrialisation and exports is tremendous. In the village side, trade takes place in kind and not in monetary denominations. Even in some places labour is paid in kind and the Government's labour laws have no application. India's export and import trade is still largely in the hands of the foreigners and India's weakness in shipping and banking and general insurance has been largely responsible for the heavy drain on foreign exchange resources and the excessive dependence upon foreign shipping companies and banking institutions even for India's industrial development.

In a country like India where on account of poor standard of living the propensity to consume is very low the margin of savings is also low which detracts from heavy investment of Indian capital and also acts as a deterrent for massive foreign private investment. It is wrong to assume that foreign capital is waiting at our door. India is not particularly attractive to venture capital as for the several reasons stated above, high profits are not possible even if permitted by Government. Even our own tax structure as far as it goes follows the pattern of industrially developed countries and we have to explore every opportunity to induce foreign investors and attract foreign capital. There are, no doubt, adequate opportunities for industrial expansion and a potentially vast *home* market, that too in a reasonably stable economy, and if we *supplement* it by the promise of a fair deal to foreign investors we might be *able* to attract such foreign capital as is *willing* to take a long range view for its *own interest* and serve the social purpose to which the Indian capital is also subjected.

In this climate, India has had to to experiment and evolve an economic philosophy of *its own* without destroying the foundations of the existing industries and interests. The effort required the synthesis of the conflict to suit the long-term objectives of India and the methods we proposed to pursue in the economic sphere were to depend largely on cooperation from Western countries and the USSR. While these countries are politically administered under a rigid system of beliefs and cooperation amongst themselves, an allowance had to be made for frequent changes in their economic policies and institutions. India has also benefitted from the remarkable rate of progress in the economic field in West Germany following the liberal economic policies of its Economic Minister, Erhard Ludwig. We have also seen the progress under democratic socialist administration in Norway and Sweden. No doubt our approach has been pragmatic in many issues and we cannot borrow wholesale from the examples of other countries because our problems and institutions are peculiarly *our own* and, in a sense, *unique*. We have an enormous population with no outlet; an enormous magnitude of unemployment, shortage of productive land, machinery and materials. This cannot be solved by any single set of solutions. Many of Government's actions have to be dictated by the limited considerations of solving single sets of problems as may come up for solution from time to time.

II

The task of industrial development of a magnitude envisaged in the Second and Third Plans required fresh foreign investments and Government had to evolve their own development programmes in regard to such matters. At the outset all fears about the socialistic pattern of society have had to be removed. India had to be made safe and stable for massive foreign investment and the tendencies for any dis-investment which were noticed in the earlier years after the wake of Indian independence had to arrested. Indian leaders assured the foreign interests that they would take an objective view in all such matters and pleaded for their cooperation in the economic advancement of the country so that they could get over the economic stagnation that was binding the Indian masses. All the assurances made in the past to the foreign capitalists were honoured. It was explained that the amendment of Article 31 to the Constitution was made for domestic reasons and either before or after the amendment the Indian Government's attitude to foreign capital had remained the same. The foreign investor had nothing to fear in regard to his investment as a consequence of this amendment. The real test of foreign help was not the giving of *doles* but in the sharing of technical knowledge and helping India to industrialise and in sharing with India such materials that are in short supply and that will be needed badly by India to achieve the the objectives of her Planes. Aid was, expected from all sources so long as it was not tied to any political strings. On India's part there was to be no discrimination between Indian investor and foreign investor in the same industry. Facilities for repatriation of profit and capital and royalty payments would be adequately provided. There was so much to do in the whole field of industrialisation that neither the Indian industrialists nor the foreign investors need think of the expansion of one at the expense of another. Nationalisation would not be resorted to on Ideological basis but it would be done for other compelling reasons. The support lent by the Government in the constitution and working of the investment finance institutions like the Industrial Credit and Investment Corporation I.C.I.C., Industrial Development Bank and the Life Insurance Corporation.L.I.C, would be taken by the Private Sector as an indication that Goverment has been sincere to offer its help to the private Sector. Even an institution like the N.I. D.C. (National Industrial Development Corporation) was formed with a view to help the rehabilitation of industrial units in the Private Sector, like jute and textiles. There were industries like iron and steel where Government was very much interested in the expansion of the Private Sector in the field The ship-building enterprise of Scindias at Vizagapatnam was acquired by Government when it was felt that the Private Sector could not find sufficient means to develop this enterprise. As regards coal which has found place in the Public Sector in the 1956 Resolution it is to be recognised that the Government-owned railway system and the three new steel plants would be the biggest consumers of coal providing justification for augmentation of Public Sector in this field for additional requirements in the field.

The taxation system also has in-built advantages for foreign investment and foreign techniques to come to India on contract basis. The taxation rate on income in India is slightly loaded in favour of foreign investors so that they get in India far more than what they would get from their own home country or elsewhere. Even in regard to the application of company law matters the Indian law was based substantially on the law in the U.K. and also on the law in Australia and the decision of the Board of Referees will leave no cause for grievance so far as industry is concerned. The administrative organisation to implement the new company law has also been strengthened and the Indian and foreign business community need not be afraid of official delays or any rigidity in the application of laws.

Even in labour matters Government's policy was based on their responsibility for the maintenance of an increased production and profitability and labour participation in management was not encouraged to be adopted as a slogan. Job evaluation, statistical quality control and rapid technological progress and introduction of a degree of automation might be causes for fear of unemployment and might cause concern in the minds of the Indian employees but ultimately if the labour is convinced that this advance in technique would after a period of time increase his earning capacity and reduce the physical strains and other unsatisfactory conditions of employment, the Indian labourer would welcome such a move and on such enlightenment he could be associated with management. In such matters of labour relationship ultimately the human value should be regarded as a much more important concept than machine; and the economy will greatly benefit if the man behind the machine and the industry can be reckoned as important factors—which means adjustment of relationship between the employer and employee. On the whole, the labour relationship in the Indian territory has been satisfactory and there have been no major lock-outs and strikes. The Congress Party which controlled a portion of the labour corps has been loyal to overall objectives of the country and has not supported the cause of labour at the expense of the employer. The labour legislation problem of the Indian Government has been only in the direction of consolidation and refinement of existing legislation, and they have not been discriminatory to foreign investors.

On only two matters the Government was somewhat strict in the application of their laws to the foreign investors. The Government have been insisting recently of progressively opening up the capital of foreign subsidiaries for Indian participation. This move was initiated on the belief that progressively more and more Indian capital would be allowed to participate and no percentages of Indian capital would be insisted upon. Again, in the matter of employment opportunities Government desired that more and more Indians should be associated in top-posts with the management so that they may be enabled to have a training in executive and technical fields.

III

The Government of Nehru took a number of importont economic decisions in the course of 17 years. The most important decision was the enactment of an amendment to Article 31 (2) of the Indian Constitution which made the amount of compensation paid to a party for Government acquisition of his property not justiciable in a court of law. The need for enacting such a legislation was simple in that Government wanted to pay some compensation for taking possession of the property and that the amount of compensation should not be impugned in a court of law. The approach of the Government in this respect was with a view to undertake agrarian reforms and also to interfere in industrial undertakings wherever they failed to satisfy social needs. The progress of Governmental action in the industrial field has been slow but even the small action was enough to create fears and suspicion in the minds of the foreign investors in the country and abroad.

The nationalisation of the State Bank of India and subsequently the Life Insurance Companies also put the Government into a position to have to explain to the investing public their intentions both in the short and long term objectives. The fact that Prime Minister made a special statement on the role of foreign capital in 1948 and again in 1949 and later on in 1956, indicates that the Government of India set a value on foreign capital providing a certain amount of stimulus to India's industrial development. Perhaps the most important consideration weighing with the Government was that they not only welcomed the participation of foreign capital but also their technical know-how which was lacking in the country to a deplorable extent.

The Industrial Resolution of 1956 should be considered as a very highly important document which not only set out in broad terms the break-down of the private and public sector but also it defined the role of the state after reiterating the objectives of the socialistic pattern of society, namely, "It is always open to the State to undertake any type of industrial production." It also envisaged a certain amount of operation for the private Sector and also *coordination* of industrial activity in both the sectors. The 1956 Resolution explains that in appropriate cases privately owned units may be promoted to produce an item falling within the first category to meet their own requirements or as by-products. "There will be ordinarily no bar to small privately-owned units undertaking production such as the making of launches and other light craft, generation of power for local needs and small-scale mining." Further, heavy industries in the Public Sector may obtain some of their requirements of lighter components from the Private Sector, while the Private Sector in turn would rely for many of its needs on the Public Sector. The same principle would apply with a greater force to the relationship between large-scale and small-scale industries.

The 1956 Resolution has been described by some observers as an *economic* constitution for industrialisation based upon its political counterpart, namely, the Constitution of India. This is so because it is linked with the Constitution by re-affirmation in the Preamble of justice, Liberty, Equality and Fraternity, cited from its "Directive Principles of State Policy", that the State shall strive to promote the welfare of the people by securing and protecting as effectively as it may the social order in which justice--social, economic and political—shall inform all the institutions of the national life." Six principles are enumerated, two of which have special significance—

(1) Ownership and control of the material resources of the community are so distributed as best to serve the common good; and,

(2) that the operation of the economic system does not result in the concentration of wealth and means of production to the common detriment.

It is significant to know that while reference is made to Parliament's acceptance of the socialistic pattern of society, the Resolution emphasises that industrial policy like other policies must be governed by the fairly definite principles and directions contained in the Constitution. There have been significant improvements in the 1956 Resolution as compared to the earlier policy of 1948 and the following conclusions are pertinent having relevance to the Public and Private Sectors.

(i) Greater emphasis is to be placed on Government's development of an expanded Public Sector.

(ii) An increasing proportion of the activities of the Private Sector will be developed along cooperative lines.

(iii) while Private industry will be permitted

to develop along with State-owned undertakings, in all the three categories defined in the 1956 Resolution private industry will be subjected to overall State regulation so that it may not get advantages detrimental to the welfare of the people.

(iv) Private enterprise is allowed to enter the industrial field reserved for state development if it *is found* that exclusive jurisdiction will retard development or otherwise the national interest.

(v) With the exception of one or two industries dealing with public utilities and national resources, India has abandoned overall programme to nationalise private industry falling within the Public Sector.

The essential point to be noted is that Private Sector has been given an honourable place in the nation's economy and its future role and justification exists provided it is considered advantageous to the notion's interests. As a matter of proof of Government's honest intentions the three foreign-controlled oil refineries and the Indian-controlled steel plants that were authorised after the State had assumed exclusive responsibility are examples where, in the national interest, they have been allowed to continue in their own field. The significant omission in the 1956 Resolution as compared to the 1948 Resolution was the previlage of review of the privatelyowned industries at the end of over 10 years, the review to determine whether they should be acquired by the State or not. A final assurance that there will be no nationalisation of private industry falling within the first category is the statement, namely, where there existed in the same industry both privately-and publicily-owned units it would continue to be the policy of the State to give fair and non-discriminatory treatment to both of them. Government have also declared that they would provide finance for all legitimate development in the private sector. Private enterprise, therefore, has been given an opportunity to *justify* its existence by making itself as a worth-while entity and its future position will depend upon good behaviour during the years ahead. Private enterprise is expected to supplement the effort of the State and will also have the opportunity to develop either on its own or with the State participation.

On the whole, the public reaction to the 1956 Resolution was wholly favourable and prices on the stock exchange recorded a moderate rise. The Tata's stocks advanced to Rs. 6 per share. An official of the Tata Brothers welcomed the announcement "whereby units in the Private Sector can be allowed to develop with freedom consistent with the targets and objectives of the Plan."

The 1956 Resolution has no special section of foreign investment but it mentions that the policy of the Prime Minister before Parliament on April 6, 1949, still applies. The role of foreign capital in the industrial development of the country has some implications. Historically, foreign capital came to be identified with foreign dominotion. And even after independence, the fear that it would canstitute a stranglehold on India's economic life and impair our own freedom of action was to be allayed. Possibly this fear arose out of suspicion and antipathy towards certain countries from which investment as a rule has been forthcoming. The

Indian capitalists also entertained suspicion that their own scope for development would be retarded because foreign capital was more advantageously placed than the Indian capital in point of technique and resources

The principal instruments which Governmnet used to achieve their economic objectives were :—

(1) The Industries (Development & Regulation) Act, 1954.

(2) Import and Export Control Orders and the Essential Commodities Supplies and Distribution Act.

(3) The Indian Tariff Act.

(4) The Sea Customs Tariff.

(5) The Central Excise Act.

(6) The Indian Income-Tax Act; and other enactments like Wealth Tax Act, Estate Duty Act, Gifts Tax Act, etc.

(7) The Companies Act, 1956.

(8) The Control of Capital Issues.

(9) Various legislative enactments relating to the financial institutions, like the Reserve Bank of India, the State Bank of India, Industrial Finance Corporation, Industrial Development Bank and Re-Finance Corporation, etc.

(10) The Industrial Disputes Act, 1956.

In an under-developed country like India, the objective of a sound taxation policy had to be defined and formulated not only to produce a sizable addition to public revenues to suit the Plan effort but also to provide for sufficient *incentives* for large earnings and savings. India, like most Western countries, has been in the grip of a vicious circle as far as progressive taxation is concerned—tax evasion and tax avoidance in a large scale. Even the notion of what constitutes "ineome" for tax purposes underwent a number of changes as a result of numerous kinds of concessions which Government have had to devise to promote industrial development on a *selective* basis. As more and more development took place, it was increas ingly felt necessary to stimulate investment in selected fields by institution of such fiscal devices as liberal depreciation allowance, tax holiday, system of development rebate, re-adjustment of the tax rate to encourage foreign investment, etc. Later, as the industrial base became widened, the policy of selective preference of priority industries became more and more narrowed and the concept of urgent development of some "special" industries as against "general" industrial development became more and more insistent, while simultaneously changes have had to be made in the tax structure with a view to make the tax yield progressively more responsive to increased incomes and facilitate an orderly development of the economy with due regard to the social objectives which the Government have adopted. The tax structure had also to aim at an efficient system of collection and general increase in industrial and agricultural production and an equitable pattern of income and wealth which would ensure a *balanced* progress. Such a system required a strengthening of incentives to work and to save, and was to be evolved both on short-term and long-term basis. The Budget of 1957 which contained the above ingredients of the tax policy stipulated that the standard rate of tax on earned income and a differential rate for taxation of un-earned income, coupled with a tax on wealth and a tax on expenditure, would give a better basis for assessment of tax liability in respect of higher income regions and would also help Government to close progressively the loopholes of tax evasion and corrosion of tax base. This budget also brought down the exemption limit for tax liability with a view to reach the masses on a broad net. This budget and similar others that followed also contained measures for gift tax, estate duty and capital gains tax.

The Budget of 1957 was defended by Prime Minister Nehru immediately after presentation and nowhere in the annals of financial history has a Prime Minister stood up and defended a course of action adopted by the Finance Minister. It was so because the proposals were the proposals of the *Government* and not of the Finance Minister's private domain. Since then the burden of defence and development has been growing and more avenues for receipts have to be found. Time was of the greatest urgency and the question was how best to distribute the heavy burdens arising out of the process of development. We had to learn from the experience of others and try to create our own policy having regard to the background of the country and the institutions already available and to be newly created to suit the genius of the Indian people. Rightly or wrongly, the country had accepted a planned effort and it was embarking on a bold programme of steel plants, big machine plants etc., and this planning process thought of two or three *generations* ahead, as some of these plants would take five to ten years for construction. Therefore, the sooner we got them done, even at a heavy cost, the better it was, as delaying it would only add to our burden and make it a somewhat longer burden. The Plan effort also indicated to the country as well as to the world outside, not only the need for self-reliance for raising the resources by way of taxation but also our determination to go ahead in an orderly way. Nehru declared : "It is an important thing to make it clear to ourselves and to others that we are determined to go ahead and to fulfil the pledge we took to our people. The tax burden felt by every tax-payer makes him realise that he is a partner in the national activity." These taxation proposals struck out a new line of approach and scores of budgets of this type would have to be done before socialism could come into this country. The Budget of 1957 took the country out of the old rut of the old budgets and pointed out to the "new" direction which was a desirable direction. Many changes were taking place in the world and our country was new to economic development and heavy resources were involved. Even in the case of Soviet Union, which has had nearly 40 years of experience, a great many things have happened and the burdens the people of that great country have carried had been tremendous.

In a poor country like India the fiscal measures constituted not only a means for sound economic growth but also had to provide for the greatest advance towards economic equality and positive social improvement. Even in the field of indirect taxation the burden was inevitable, in view of the process of development that was taking place in the country, and funds could not be collected without calling for such sacrifices from all sections of the community. There were also special and compelling reasons for applying some restraint on consumption in order to check inflationary pressure and to stimulate exports. Over a period of years the stagnancy of public revenue relatively to national income, which was a bottleneck from the point of view of further development, would be overcome. Thus, the structural changes in the tax system were also made with a view to make it more progressive in terms of returns.

The peculiar conditions of planned development for a number of years resulting in sharp incrases in the general price level and increase in the prices of some essential commodities, called for adjustment in incomes since the margin of tolerance in a poor country like India was limited. Government were, therefore, forced to keep a vigilant watch over the general indexes of wholesale prices and whenever any increases took place there was a need for utmost discipline in every sphere of activity.

In the investment field Government's policy was also to make a shift of emphasis from low-priority to high-priority industries. One of the weaknesses of the Indian economy has been that substantial portion of the community's savings are diverted towards industries of low priority, quick speculative gains through purchase and sale of urban housing and the hoarding of commodities in short supply. From this point of view, the savings of the community have to be guided into proper investment channels. Therefore, a number of steps had to be taken to ensure a sound investment policy supported by fiscal, monetary and institutional agencies. The Reserve Bank has annonced that it would ensure that credit for *all* legitimate purposes would be available in the country. The accent on monetary and credit policy had also to be integrated with a realistic rate of interest which reflected adequately the real cost of the capital to the economy. At the same time, the supply of the credit should be made adequate to meet the needs of the growth. Working on this basis, Government have taken a number of measures to stimulate the growth of savings on one hand, and at the same time, to make them flow into medium term and long-term finance for industrial development. As a result of the three Plans, opportunities, for investment at a higher profitability rate were made available and gross sales and grossprofits of the companies were also progressively increasing. Planning involved in the monetary field a dear-money rate which would necessarily reduce the yield from old issues, and operate a "bear" factor in the stock exchange. With a view to neutralise these effects, the under-writing functions of the specialised financial institutions were augmented in recent years. Government have, therefore, to operate selective credit control with a view to promote the growth of industry on the one hand and underline the needs for investment in high-priority industries on the other. On the fiscal side, some tax concessions were provided to accelarate the pace of industrial development such as tax credit certificate, tax rebate for additional production and on exports. Tax concessions occupied an important place in the economy with a view to give the private sector units relief and strengthen the reserves and augment the capacities of the corporate sector. The various measures envisaged for better flow of medium and long-term finance in industrial development include the creation of a number of financial institutions like the Industrial Development Bank, Unit Trust, etc., which are intended to strengthen and broaden the framework of the capital market as a source of supply of funds to industry.

It will be thus seen that monetary and fiscal policies were being woven into the industrial policy. There were, no doubt, seasonal difficulties caused by the expansion and contraction of bank credits during the busy and slack seasons which is a peculiar phenomenon in the agricultural country of the size like India and the liquidity position was rapidly changing and Government have had to be vigilant to come forward to make changes from time to time to suit the monetary requirements of the various sectors of the economy. On the whole, the economic boom created by the expansion of activity as a result of the pressure on funds both in the monetary and non-monetary sectors had been visible and it had to be regulated by various instruments available before the Reserve Bank and the Government. And all these instruments had to be integrated and supported by fiscal policies. The Government had also to assist the Reserve Bank in the regulation of credit by enforcing anti-inflationary policy and this called for frequent adjustments in the fiscal side in indirect taxes like import and excise duties.

Money supply, supply of funds to the needy sectors. direction of savings into productive investment channels, checking the tendency to hoard agricultural commodities and industrial raw-materials like raw cotton, were the main aims and objectives on the monetary side. The fiscal policy was integrated with the monetary policy to neutralise unhealthy market forces. And over and above these changes, adjustments of rates and articles to be subjected to duties and adjustments in the prevailing rates of interest became unavoidable to keep pace with the supply and demand conditions.

The overall effects of the economic policy have resulted in expansion of activity in all sectors. The national income in India in real terms was estimated to have recorded a rise of 7.5% during 1964-'65 as against 4.5% in 1963-64. Similarly, the *per capita* income in real terms has increased by 4.9% during 1964-'65, the overall annual increase during first four years of the Third Plan being 1.8%. The industrial base of the country has also been widened during the last two years of the Third Plan and the rate of growth of economy in 1964-'65 was estimated to be 8% as against 4.5% in 1963-'64.

There was also a remarkable progress in the resources mobilisation for meeting the Third Plan requirements and the ratio of taxation to national income increased from 9.6% at the end of 1960-'61 to 14% in March, 1965. The rate of savings also has reached the level of 11% as in March. 1965. The amount of capital raised by the companies has also registered an increase. Private imports of capital equipment have also increased. Gross profit and gross sales have also been going up and many foreign collaboration agreements have been entered into. Thus, there has been an overall increase in production, imports, exports, *gross* profits of the companies, *gross* sales of the companies and an increase in the results of development in the infra-structure of the economy, the rate of growth in industry, the rate of increase in national income and in the ratio of taxation to national income. The above analysis will show that broadly the economic health of the country has been sound in the sense that in terms of social and welfare overheads there has been much progress. There may be some defects arising from lack of institutional support, lack of cohesion in the administrative set—up and lack of overall implementation of the Plan both in the Centre and the State sectors. and lastly, the existence of social and economic habitat outside the orbit of the planning organisation. The sense of planning that is commonly understood in Russia cannot be transplanted in the Indian soil. Government cannot also overtly direct the Private Sector units to invest their surpluses into further production of 'desirable' industries. Fortunately, we have a democratic Constitution and a system of free enterprise. Though our policy envisages regulation of industrial growth, it cannot result in unrestricted growth in the normal sense of the term as it applies to the United Kingdom, the U.S.A. or the West Germany. Government can only create the climate and it is for the Private Sector to take advantage of it.

On the whole, the economic administration of the country during the last 17 years enjoyed a period of stability and was made to subserve the social and economic objectives of democracy. The tools and institutions which Nehru and his colleagues used for the economic transformation of the country were multi-sided and aimed at enlarging the opportunities for new entrants in the fields of industry and commerce while encouraging the existing ones to play their proper role in the economy. For the new entrants a lot of spade work has been done by Government initiative to clear the way and slowly and imperceptively a new *class* of people has been coming up on the surface of the body politic. The planning effort of the Government no doubt resulted in lopsided development of the economy in some segments; and two main trends of economic concentration of power have come to stay even though the policies aimed at socialistic objectives. This was because the means of production had come to be owned historically by a group of firms who benefitted from the licensing system of the Government and who had the *ability* and *experience* in those fields. Simultaneously, a new class of people was also emerging with new product-wise concentration because these products have come to be produced for the first time in the country. These situations required a continuous watch to serve the social good of the community and impelled the Government to adopt regulatory measures in the large interests of the country and in accordance with their professions of socialist objectives.

But from the overall point of view Government brought to bear an integrated approach towards the programme of industrialisation by noticing the inextricable connection between transport—railways, road transport and shipping—and industrialisation and to the problem of supplying the people with goods and services which they badly needed. Sometimes physical controls would be necessary for economic planning; sometimes Government have to take into account factors in the fiscal policy, monetary policy, investment policy and also policies in regard to other matters of an administrative character which have a bearing on all these. Government had also to take an overall view and a *coordinated* action in several key sectors which had inter-connection amongst themselves such as coal development, iron and steel development, port and railways, expansion schemes and developing ancillary industries which used basic raw-materials like steel etc. Government also had to evolve a coordinated power programme which was an implicit condition for the achievment of the industrial target. While making such programme, allowance had to be made for pattern of power development to provide for regional grids etc.

In some cases advance planning had to be done in regard to power and transport facilities which involved long periods of construction. The importance of investment in human resources was also not neglected as it was felt that technical eduaction and scientific sesearch for agricultural, industrial and other developments would languish if plans are not formulated in terms of requirements of the economy in various sectors. The Planning Commission appointed in September, 1955, an Engineering Personnel Commitee to assess the requirements of engineers and artisans and as a result a number of enginneering institutions was set up. The Coordination Committee under the Education Ministry had also considered the requirements of the various Ministries and the requirements of the State Governments and the Private Sector and made some recommendations foro pening up new institutions and provision of more facilities in scientific and technical education.

An overal view for foreign exchange requirements and servicing of foreign debts had to be taken for the requirements of the various sectors of the economy including defence needs. While new industries were coming up, a large maintenance gap was also emerging in regard to raw-materials, components and spares needed by the existing industries. With the expansion of domestic capacity for machine building and in the context of reduced foreign aid more and more of the equipment needed by the new industries would have to come from domestic resources; and while this process might involve some delay it was essential that the domestic machine building and other capital goods industries should be assured of timely and adequate supplies of the raw-materials and components needed by them. In general, our dependence on foreign aid both for development and for covering the maintenance gap has increased and this has come as a limiting factor in the pace of industrialsation. Most priorty proejcts are now of a kind which involve a specialised know-how as well as heavy foreign exchange expenditure and it takes time to arrange them. The relatively slow progress of steel castings and forgings, machine tools in the Private

Sector' ball-bearings and special steels is largely explained by the delays and difficulties in arranging foreign collaboration. Free foreign exchange has become available to a very limited extent and is mostly used for high-priority projects. In this context there were increasing difficulties in the starting up of new enterprises both in the Private and Public Sectors unless the necessary foreign exchange was available out of aid, suppliers' credit, equity participation or under Rupee arrangement. This by itself acted as a serious retarding factor. Even when aid became available, allocation to Private Sector projects was often made in the form of foreign exchange loans from I.F.C., I.C.I.C. or foreign agencies like C.D.F.C. and this involved protracted negotiations with these bodies. In respect of suppliers' credits, agreements have to be entered into between Indian importers and foreign suppliers. Since most foreign exchange allocations for capital goods are tied to particular sources of supply, our entrepreneurs are often forced to obtain their equipment from an unfamiliar source and this meant some additional exploration. In short, the difficulties arising from the shortage of foreign exchange have acted as a time-consuming factor in the development of industries.

The Industries (Development and Regulation) Act, 1954, which controls the Private Sector has been, by and large, administered liberally but in the process of encouraging new units to come into production, there was implicitly an attempt to prevent the already existing licensed units from expanding output in excess of licensed capacity or utilise it for manufacture of new products. Sometimes speedy action was not taken against those who failed to take effective steps to utilise their licenses. Other policy decisions like the restrictions on inter-company investments, absence of relief from double taxation, unrealistic export obligations prescribed for new units in some industries, have also tended to impede investment in certain industries.

The recommendations of the various Finance Commissions set up under the Constitution at the end of each five-year period also determined the financial relationship between the States and the Centre. The Budget of the Government which formed the annual feature both in the State as well well as in the Centre, was also the occasion for such financial review and various aspects of the economy came under the influence of such review.

On the whole, there was financial and economic stability arising out of political stability in the country. The import and export policies of Government had also been laid down in advance for the information of the business community and they imparted a measure of stability to the economy of the country and provided the guide-lines for industrialisation, foreign investment and technical know-how. Government also approached the problem of planning with an integrated frame of thinking with a view to bear upon a close coordination of development in major sectors of the economy like transport, mineral development, ports and power, and also in the States. The Private Sector which enjoyed initiative in certain basic industries were allowed to expand but there was a constant regulation by Government not only on the production but also on price and distribution. The excessive dependence of Private Sector of Government for import of raw-materials and capital goods and foreign exchange allocations may have reduced the potentialities of its growth to a considerable extent. The taxation policy of the Government may have also limited the availability of the investment funds for the Private Sector who became excessively dependent upon Government institutions for equity financing. The overall effect of all these policies was that while on the one hand Government Public Sector undertakings, completely devoid of associations with any Private Sector firm arose out of Government funds, the Private Sector industries were having difficulties in their growth and expansion due to *excessive* dependence on Government. And on the whole, there was a straining and curtailment of the total resources available for the development of the country. The adverse effects of these *kinds* of stunted growth in the economy were felt whenever agricultural shortages took place and exports also did not go up to the desired level. Thus, the growth of the national income was greatly retarded, affecting the overall savings and investible resources; and foreign aid and foreign capital not only became necessary for the maintenance of import and inflow of technical know-how, but also they have come to stay as a permanent feature for some years to come. Thus, the implementation of policies required a flexible and day-to-day adjustment between Government and the various sections of the people and economy.

The States have also emerged as owners of Public Sector undertakings in their own field. The slow rate of increase in agricultural production due to experiments in agrarian reforms and failures in monsoon have resulted in the worsening of their way and means position and as a result the price level of the country has shot up to disproportionate levels. In an economy where population has been increasing and production of agricultural and industrial products has not been keeping pace to a satisfactory level, the take-off stage for the industrial development is bound to suffer a set-back and will be definitely postponed.

Such occasions serve as a timely warning for a continuous review of the basic economic and industrial policies of the Government of India and the State Governments. A number of remedies have to be suggested, such as the slowing down of the pace of the Plan, the re-arranging of priorities, certain remedial measures to remove all fears and suspicion in the minds of Indian population and foreign investors and the constant revision in the present taxation and fiscal policies of the Government without abandoning the socialistic objectives. Government's measures calculated to dissipate economic concentration of power and also to reduce inequalities of income and wealth by measures like the amendments to the Indian Companies Act and fiscal policies and such others have also to be reviewed in the light of the long-term objectives to be achieved in a *democratic* way and not by any narrow consideration.

While many criticisms may have some value and may provide an occasion for a review it should be clear that we should not foresake the essential objectives on which the Constitution of the Government has been embodied and several other "forward" steps taken by Government in this direction.

The Democratic values at the Government and Party level will have to be adhered to at *any cost*; *means* here democracy should be construed as a means to an end and not as an end in itself. The people of India should not be treated as mere mechanical units but regarded as dignified human beings. The traditions of culture and social value will have to be enhanced and peace and stability in the country assured. This is possible only by maintaining a healthy party system within the framework of the Constitution and the Opposition parties functioning within the framework of the Constitution to serve the basic objectives of a democratic Government.

The methods of working of Government may differ but the strategy and plan of the overall objectives of the planning effort should be clear to everybody including the rulers and the governed. If a good Government comes to be identified as an instrument for welfare and a progressive Government, by and large, there will be stability in the country and measures taken towards that end should be taken as good measures. The economic objectives may be only an instrument for the survival of political democracy but even here there are very many limitations towards achieving the final objectives such as availability of resources both in men and material, the large arrears of work to be done and the long interval of time that will be required in doing away the evils of the past. At any rate, the potentiality of human individual has not been tapped to a very large extent simply because the time has been short and the area of opportunities has not been widened. The country has been subjected to foreign domination for very many centuries and the work of re-building India has to be a very long and continuous process and cannot be done in a short span of time. Similarly, the absorption capacity of the people has to be improved by a number of educative and infra-structure improvements. For instance, the mental horizon of the citizens has to be enlarged by educational values and training. The land resources of the country have to be harnessed not only with a view to adopt modern equipment and scientific improvements in agriculture but also to implement these practices in "new areas". The industrial needs of the country have been broad-based, but their absorption capacity has to be enriched by adoption of research and exploitation of new methods on a commercial scale. The failure of the Third Plan, particularly in the agricultural sector, reminds us that our efforts have to be renewed in a special way to meet the food requirements of the rising population. Even in the industrial sector there remains much un-utilised capacity in most of the engineering industries and traditional industries. Thus, we have to avoid an atmosphere of mutual recrimination between the various sections of the community and also increase the scope of cooperation in new fields. Once the psychological crisis of confidence comes to stay in the minds of many sections of the people, many new problems may arise, and even the old and settled problems like the concept of mixed economy, will be questioned and the foundations of industrial growth shaken.

What the country needs is overall production and both the Public and Private Sectors must function as one unit for the national good. There should be an increasing appreciation of the difficulties facing the country on both sides and the emphasis should be made more on production than on regulation. A definite schedule of priorities, long-term, mid-term and short-term, should be prepared for implementation in all sectors of the economy. It is time for the Private Sector to realise that the capital market of the country has to undergo changes on account of the increase in the bank rate and the dear-money policy arising out of the concept of planning in the country, and many old issues have to 'adjust' themselves and get absorbed in the new set of things. Government have created a number of institutions for equity finance and some of the industries are already drawing assistance from such institutions. The growing needs of the Government for funds for the Plan effort make a chance of reduced taxation less in the future and the business community which benefits largely from such planning efforts has to reconcile itself with this position.

It is time that business community in India makes an introspection and adapts itself to the new requirements of the country. The businessmen have been patriotic enough in the past and have financed that National Party for the freedom movement. Now they know the need of the hour is unity and production. If there is disunity in any section of the community it will only subvert the financial, economic stability of the country. On the other hand, nothing has happened in a democracy without agitation. India is the only country between Egypt and Japan where there is political stability and a democratic system and a Government committed to the amelioration effort with the cooperation of *all* sections of the community in a planned and systematic way. The problem of security for the people, therefore, is closely allied to the problem of overcoming scarcity and no Government can last in any country if they do not aim for an affluent society.

The Government have taken many steps to protect and expand the Private Sector, and the private industrialists should take advantage of these steps especially the modernisation programme of jute and textiles which are losing heavily in the export market. The Indian industrialists have also to take advantage of research and exploitation of such research methods on commercial scale for the advantage of the community. In India, there has been no consultancy organisation between Government and the private industrialists on a regular basis as the Weekly Thursday meeting between the Great Five and the Chancellor of the Exchequer in U.K. A number of voluntary institutions of the type which London has developed, like the London Stock Exchange or the Union Issues or Merchant Bankers in the City of London, is yet to come in the country. A voluntary institution which includes in its membership only firms who can produce quality goods and accept regulations for the social good of their own is yet to come. The labour also has not received a proper deal from the businessmen both in the shape of rewards for their labour as well as in management. In other countries, consistent with high standards of integrity and tradition of honourable service to the business community, many voluntary bodies have come to stay and they exercise a degree and range of control over the private sector which is hardly known in this country, but which if fully known would provide a meeting ground for determining many phases of public policy. If we could leave everything to Government's initiative for regulation without businessmen themselves organising or reforming, the process of administration will be long and strenuous. Therefore, the compulsion of our accepted social objectives and economic policies renders the administration difficult and time-consuming affair. Therefore, the Private Sector has to adapt itself to the changing needs of the country and it must not waste its time in fighting a lost battle with the Government when opportunities for investment and expansion are so many in a planned economy such as that we are having at present. The Indian businessman has, therefore, a two-fold task at present, namely, that he has to produce standard goods at reasonable price and also serve the social good of the community. Time lost cannot be gained and in this common endeavour every one will have to hurry up.

EPILOGUE

One major event took place in Nehru's life-time in October, 1962, which seemed to cut at the roots of Nehru's policy of co-existence and peace and prosperity for every nation. This was the unprovoked Chinese aggression against India in October, 1962, and this was unilaterally withdrawn by the Chinese in December, 1962. India attempted to get the Indo-Chinese conflict solved by agreeing to the mediation of a group of five countries, headed by Ceylon, called the Colombo Powers, and a solution was suggested by them which was accepted by India without reservations while the Chinese made some stipulations. Further talks between India and China were to be held after an initial agreement on the major suggestions made by the Colombo Powers. In view of the Chinese attitude, further talks between India and China could not be held. At this time of Chinese attack there had been vociferous opposition in this country to the ideal of non-alignment. International observers watched whether India under Nehru would deviate from this ideal and take up to some kind of alignment with more powerful allies for the sake of protecting the territorial integrity of India. Many smaller nations which looked up to India for counsel in their international problems also watched with interest whether there would be a shift in the Indian non-alignment policy.

There were, no doubt, many arguments for making such a general shift. India was not well-equipped with weapons and trained in modern arts of warfare. Her borders stretched over a distance of 1500 miles from the Hindukush down to the NEFA and no physical protection over such a vast area was possible. In the case of Pakistan, she was already a member of the SEATO and the NATO and her defences were, by agreement with the participating countries, looked after by her "allies"

Even in such a period of trial, India *under* Nehru maintained a strict non-alignment but she sent military missions to the United States and to the USSR and East European countries for securing arms aid. Although the Chinese had withdrawn unilaterally from the Indian territory, the future will still uncertain. Nehru was keen to contain the Chinese war within the frontiers and he strove to keep it within limits and not spread outside the *Indian fontiers.* While he sought for aid from friendly countries, he believed that the Indian defences could be better protected by making preparations in a more systematic way by strengthening the industrial base of India for defence purposes. He believed that while friendly help was essential, he should not attempt to create groups in world politics by aligning with one set of countries against another. Remarkably enough the world has carried on for well-nigh 20 years without a major world war and any move at this time of history in favour of a change for an alignment with some powerful countries would only jeopardise the ideals of world peace and world unity. The urge for India developing her industrial base became more urgent and insistent as the Chinese constituted a potential threat in the future. The methods of fighting the enemy in the cold climate and the opening of transport facilities at very high altitudes in the Himalayas by construction of roads had to be done only with the assistance of the advanced friendly countries. The long-term problem was that the potential threat remained and this could be solved only by building more factories in India for producing equipments for modern warfare. For this purpose India would need trained personnel from all sources including the U.S.A., U.K., U.S.S.R., Canada and Australia. The problem was not one of equipping, but how soon we would equip ourselves and build these new factories and train our own personnel. Thus, the policy of non-alignment which India under Nehru had pursued so vigorously in the past, was further *re-affirmed* when the Chinese threat took place. Non-alignment did not mean non-participation in world affairs. It was a kind of dynamic neutrality, serving the cause of world peace and interfering in international affairs where justice and objectivity ought to prevail. It was something of a kind of assertion of moral force over the physical strength of one country or any group of countries. It meant friendship with *all* and co-existence with *every* system of ideology or *form* of Government. It had been given to Prime Minister Nehru not only to preach this ideal for others but also live by this ideal when the country was subjected to the Chinese aggression, even though he and his country have had to face insult and humiliation at the hands of a very powerful neighbour like China who tried to be friendly with India in the past.

Nehru's regime no doubt saw the failure of the policy in India's relationship with the Chinese but the future events carried a message of hope for the Indian people. One year after Nehru's death India was subjected to another aggression—from Pakistan during the regime of Shri Lal Bahadur Shastri. The people of India from all parts of the country rose to one nation and warded off the attack. Again, during the darkest time of the food crisis, in the later half of 1965 and 1966, India received many offers of help from all countries of the world. This symbolised the victory of this crusading spirit of peace and world cooperation. The fruits of Nehru's toil came to be reaped in the years to come.

II

The era of Nehru was singularly blessed with a number of men of towering stature, equally important as Nehru was. They had risen from the ranks, struggled with the common man for the liberation of the country and worked with Gandhiji in good team spirit. They were essentially men of character and sometimes their extraordinary love for the country and for the people of India forced them to make huge sacrifices for the sake of the national interest. Nehru could not have come to this level of leadership without some of these leaders like Rajan Babu, C.R. and Subhash and later, Jai Prakash, voluntarily sacrificing their career in the country. Gandhiji played a great part in the moulding of the policies of the Congress Party and remained outside the Governmental machinery even after Independence. He was not even a four anna member of the Congress

After Nehru resumed leadership of the Government after 1950, he was helped by a team of Ministers and officials to whom credit should be given for the re-building task. The integration of the Indian States and the organisation of the services were brought about solely due to the leadership of Mr. Patel, and his able lieutenant, V. P. Menon. The Foreign Services and the organisation of the various Ambassadorial ties with foreign countries were done by officers like Girija Shankar Bajpai and N. Raghava Pillai and K.P.S. Menon. The image of India and Nehru's poticies were projected outside India consistently by leaders like N. Gopalaswamy Ayyengar, Shri V. K. Krishna Menon, Dr. S. Radhakrishnan, Srimati Vijailakshmi Pandit and Dr. Rajendra Prasad.

In the economic sphere, Dr. C. D. Deshmukh was responsible for the nationlisation of the Life Insurance Companies, while during Dr. John Mathai's stewardship of Finance Ministry, the State Bank was taken over by Government.

On the food side, the control measures were lifted by Shri Rafi Ahmed Kidwai and there was a sense of relief everywhere after the de-control measures. Shri S. K. Patil was largely responsible for the American aid on a massive scale on the food front.

The work of the Planning Commission in the first 10 years fell largely upon a group of planners headed by Sir V.T. Krishnamachari. He continued to be the Deputy Chairman of the Planning Commission for about 10 years and the successes of the First Five Year Plan, especially in the agricultural sector of the economy, were due to indefatigable industry and the able assistance he got from a number of officials like Shri K.C. Neogi, Shri G.L. Nanda, Sardar Tarlok Singh of the Indian Civil Service and Dr. J. J. Anjaria. The technique of planning has now been developed into a cult and this is largely due to the personal interest taken by Prime Minister Nehru.

In the State field, two important Chief Ministers come to the forefront whenever questions of communal harmony or economic planning were taken up. They were Shri B.C. Roy of West Bengal and Shri Govind Ballabh Pant of U.P. Later, Shri Morarji

Desai, who was also the Chief Minister of undivided Bombay and who played a very important part in the following up of Gandhian and Nehru's policies, came to the Centre along with Pantji who also held the office of Home Minister for a considerable period in addition to the U.P. State's Chief Ministership.

In the economic field, both in the industry and finance, the policies of Nehru came to be handled by Shri T.T. Krishnamachari after 1954. During his regime, the Industrial Policy Resolution of 1956 was given a shape. He was also the first Finance Minister in India who gave a turn to the taxation system of the Government with a view to achieve an egalitarian society based on socialistic principles. The emergence of India as a country in tempo of industrial development happened during his regime as Industry and Finance Minister when he embarked on bold programmes of steel, heavy engineering, oil and petrochemical complexes. It was during his period that India was able to project its industrial and trade picture in the councils of the world especially in organisations like the GATT and the International Monetary Fund and the World Bank and a number of other Western and East European countries including Japan. During this period, the country witnessed the rising tempo of industrial collaboration and foreign equity participation. India began to get help from Western countries not only in the shape of capital goods but also in the sharing of technical know-how in which Indians were trained subsequently and are now in a position to take more responsibility for designing industrial establishments.

Special incentives in the shape of fiscal reliefs were given to the foreign industrialists and technicians who came to India very frequently. The country was thus prepared in his stewardship of the Finance Ministry to receive more foreign business and industrial delegations. Even when the country was subjected to external aggression in 1962 by China, he was specially sent by Prime Minister Nehru to make arrangements for Western collaboration with our defences if such a contingency arose.

Later, when he filled up the office of the Finance Minister in 1962, he introduced a number of fiscal and monetary reforms and refinements in the existing systems which were found necessary to promote a sound investment policy and implement the plan both on the resources side and also to arrest the inflationary pressures created by the Plan. He was thus responsible for forging an integrated monetary andfiscal policy and weaving it into the general pattern of the industrial policy of the countrya nd also in larger plan framework. These changes called for frequent adjustments in a number of fields like the taxation system, customs and excise tariff, control over distribution and price of commodities, and lastly, restriction of essential imports which constituted a drain on the already scarce foreign exchange, and also rationing on a strict basis of foreign aid amongst the competing claimants. The economic system was thus made flexible to accommodate the adjustments that had to be made in the various segments and planning in general as well as in particular fields of development like power and selective industrial development gained an impetus.

He brought upon the plan programmes an integrated approach into all sectors of the economy and strove to accelerate the pace of industrialisation in certain sectors which constitute the hard core of the Plan. Some of the short-term measures which he introduced to discipline the excesses in certain fields and also such measures as voluntary disclosure of concealed income, created a lot of heat and controversy. By and large, judged from the long-term aspect and the inhibitions that the economy was suffering already, these measures could be regarded as salutary. During this regime also the emphasis on development of selected industries in preference to general industrial development and the enlargement of the Public Sector projects came to dominate the thinking of planners and administrators in general.

Lastly, in this task, he was helped by a well-knit team of officers like Mr. H.M. Patel, Mr. P.C. Bhattacharya, Mr. A.K. Roy, Mr. H.V.R. Iengar, Mr. Bhoothalingam, Mr. Ranganathan, Mr. B. K. Nehru, Mr. L.K. Jha, Mr. K.B. Lall, Mr. P. Govindan Nair, Mr. S. Jagannathan, and a number of other Civil Service officers.

The comments of the leading dailies in India about his achievements at that time are given below :—

The Statesman dated 2.2.1955.

"He had been a successful head of a Ministry that earlier had not always had firm guidance. To his appointment he brought practical business experience, which *inter alia* prompted him to improve the system of import licensing, long a source of vexation to businessmen. No doctrinaire, he assuaged some of the concern caused by the Industries (Development) Act, and in general administered his charge with due regard both for overall State superintendence and the requirements of the private sector. During his term of office industrial production has risen notably, the crisis in the tea industry was overcome, modernization of equipment went ahead, import policy was liberalised and steps were taken to expand exports."

Hindustan Times dated 2.2.1955.

"Can the nation afford to let go his ideas? Individuals, indeed, are expendable. In this vast country, even men of the calibre of Mr. Krishnamachari may be quite a few. The nation cannot afford to let go his broad imagination, much practical wisdom and great administrative drive. Less is known publicly perhaps of his fine achievement in building up an excellent corps of senior officers for his Ministry; he has made top-grade economic civil servants out of the common or garden variety. Above all, by his effort and example, he has given a big push forward to the industrialisation programme of the Second Five Year Plan."

The Times of India dated 14.2.1955

"After cataloguing his achievements, it states." But more important than these has been Mr. Krishnamachari's dynamic approach to the problem of industrialisation. Industry and trade found in him a friend and counsellor and a stern task-master at the same time. Likewise, he earned the respect of the foreign investor despite his strong attitude regarding Indianisation.

"He gave in the battle for socialisation an honourable place to the private sector and exercised a good deal of moderation over the administration of the Industries (Development and Regulation) Act. He spelt out the idea of *co-existence* of private and public sectors in the country's economy and was responsible for the symmetrical attitude in the issue of State control over the plan sector. Elaborating this idea, he explained symmetry meant coherent and consistent pattern of the policy making and administration which did not curb one productive economic activity in order to promote another, but would aim at the optimum level of economic development through the full play of expansionist impulse in all the sectors."

"During the past years of our working in close companionship in matters of great consequence to our country, we have sometimes differed, we have argued with each other and on a few occasions we have even had rather sharp differences. There is nothing surprising abont it because we were dealing with vital matters on which varying opinions are possible. But in the larger context, all this was of little consequence becouse we *agreed* on the major policies to be adopted, and had respect and, may I say, affection for each other. I admired your devotion to work, your broad vision and keenness of intellect. Ever since you became Minister of Finance, you brought a new and vigorous outlook to your great task and took us out of certain grooves in which we were functioning. In a period of increasing difficulty, you did a signal service to our Second Five Year Plan and to our country for whose progress this Plan is meant. I an deeply grateful to you for this and I am sure my gratitude is shared by vast numbers of people."

(Letter from the late Prime Minister Shri Nehru to Shri T.T. Krishnamachari, dt. New Dehli the 12th February, 1958).

ERRATA

Page	*Line*	*for*	*read*
1	8	1489	1948
2	13	car	scar
5	21	delete words "in the"	
5	22	insert words "in the" after the word "leaders"	
21	26	wo ld	world
21	28	made	make
32	30	after Lalithkala put)	
46	16	humality	humility
77	11	insert "be" after "to"	
78	1	Planes	Plans
78	16	Put the letters I.C·I.C. in brackets.	
78	17	Put the letters L.I.C. in brackets.	
84	19	notion	nation
97	7	o pening	opening
102	5	means	Even
102	22	insert "a" after "for"	
108	16	will	was
113	6	in addition to	after relinquishing
115	12	this	his